TABLE OF CONTENTS

BREAKFAST & BRUNCH

Deep-Dish Vegetable Quiche

- 1¼ cups biscuit baking mix
- ¼ cup (½ stick) plus 1 tablespoon butter, softened, divided
- 1½ tablespoons water
- 2 cups small broccoli florets (about ¾-inch pieces)
- 1½ cups sliced white mushrooms (4 ounces)
- 1 cup chopped red bell pepper
- ¾ cup finely chopped green onions (about 1 bunch)
- 1 cup (4 ounces) shredded Swiss cheese
- ½ cup (2 ounces) shredded sharp Cheddar cheese
- 1½ cups milk
- 3 eggs
- ½ teaspoon salt
- ⅛ teaspoon ground red pepper

1. Preheat oven to 375°F. Spray 9-inch deep-dish pie plate with nonstick cooking spray.
2. Combine baking mix, ¼ cup butter and water in small bowl; stir to form soft dough. Shape into a ball; flatten into a disc. Press dough evenly onto bottom and up sides of prepared pie plate.
3. Melt remaining 1 tablespoon butter in medium skillet over medium heat. Add broccoli, mushrooms and bell pepper; cook 2 minutes, stirring occasionally. Stir in green onions. Spoon mixture into crust; top with cheeses.
4. Whisk milk, eggs, salt and ground red pepper in medium bowl until well blended. Pour into crust.
5. Bake 40 minutes or until center is set and knife inserted into center comes out clean. Let stand 15 minutes. Cut into wedges to serve.

Makes 6 servings

Spaghetti and Vegetable Frittata

- **2 tablespoons butter, divided**
- **1 package (8 ounces) sliced white or cremini mushrooms**
- **1 cup thinly sliced leeks (white and light green parts)**
- **5 eggs**
- **⅓ cup milk**
- **3 tablespoons grated Parmesan cheese**
- **½ teaspoon salt**
- **⅛ teaspoon ground nutmeg**
- **⅛ teaspoon black pepper**
- **1 package (10 ounces) frozen chopped collard greens, thawed and squeezed dry**
- **2 cups cooked whole grain spaghetti**
- **½ cup (2 ounces) shredded mozzarella cheese**

1. Melt 1 tablespoon butter in large ovenproof skillet over medium-high heat. Add mushrooms and leeks; cook and stir 8 minutes or until lightly browned.
2. Whisk eggs, milk, Parmesan, salt, nutmeg and pepper in large bowl. Stir in collard greens, spaghetti and mushroom mixture.
3. Melt remaining 1 tablespoon butter in same skillet over medium-low heat. Add egg mixture; cover and cook 10 minutes or until top is set.
4. Meanwhile, preheat broiler. Sprinkle mozzarella over frittata; broil 5 inches from heat source 3 minutes or until golden brown. Cut into wedges to serve.

Makes 6 servings

Tip: Turn last night's dinner into tomorrow's breakfast. Cook more spaghetti than you need, measure 2 cups and place in a food storage container. If you have time while making dinner, you could even cook the vegetables in advance to give yourself an extra head start in the morning.

Spinach, Mushroom, Egg and Gruyère Rollups

- 1 tablespoon plus 4 teaspoons olive oil, divided
- 1 shallot, thinly sliced (about ½ cup)
- 1 package (5 ounces) baby spinach
- 1 clove garlic, minced
- ½ teaspoon plus ⅛ teaspoon salt, divided
- 1 package (8 ounces) cremini mushrooms, thinly sliced
- ¼ teaspoon black pepper, divided
- 2 pieces flatbread such as lavash or naan, 9½×11-inches*
- ⅔ cup shredded Grùyere or Swiss cheese
- 6 eggs
- 2 tablespoons milk
- 2 teaspoons Dijon mustard

**Various types of flatbread can usually be found in the bakery department of large supermarkets. If flatbread is unavailable, substitute large flour tortillas (fajita or burrito size).*

1. Heat 2 teaspoons oil in large nonstick skillet over medium heat. Add shallot; cook and stir 5 minutes or until softened. Add spinach; cook 2 minutes or until wilted. Add garlic and ¼ teaspoon salt; cook 1 minute, stirring frequently. Transfer to small bowl.
2. Heat 1 tablespoon oil in same skillet over medium-high heat. Add mushrooms, ¼ teaspoon salt and ⅛ teaspoon pepper; cook 6 minutes or until browned, stirring occasionally.
3. Spread half of spinach and mushrooms on each flatbread; top with cheese.
4. Whisk eggs, remaining ⅛ teaspoon salt, ⅛ teaspoon pepper, milk and mustard in large bowl until blended.
5. Heat remaining 2 teaspoons oil in same skillet over medium heat. Add egg mixture; cook about 3 minutes or until eggs are set but still moist and softly scrambled, stirring occasionally. Spread eggs over vegetables; roll up flatbread. Cut rolls in half diagonally to serve.

Makes 4 servings

Frittata Rustica

- **4 ounces cremini mushrooms, stems trimmed, cut into quarters**
- **1 tablespoon olive oil, divided**
- **½ teaspoon plus ⅛ teaspoon salt, divided**
- **½ cup chopped onion**
- **1 cup packed chopped stemmed lacinato kale**
- **½ cup halved grape tomatoes**
- **4 eggs**
- **½ teaspoon Italian seasoning**
- **Black pepper**
- **⅓ cup shredded mozzarella cheese**
- **1 tablespoon shredded Parmesan cheese**
- **Chopped fresh parsley (optional)**

1. Preheat oven to 400°F. Spread mushrooms on small baking sheet; drizzle with 1 teaspoon oil and sprinkle with ⅛ teaspoon salt. Roast 15 to 20 minutes or until well browned and tender.
2. Heat remaining 2 teaspoons oil in small (6- to 8-inch) ovenproof nonstick skillet over medium heat. Add onion; cook and stir 5 minutes or until soft. Add kale and ¼ teaspoon salt; cook 10 minutes or until kale is tender, stirring frequently. Add tomatoes; cook and stir 3 minutes or until tomatoes are soft. Stir in mushrooms.
3. Preheat broiler. Whisk eggs, remaining ¼ teaspoon salt, Italian seasoning and pepper in small bowl until well blended.
4. Pour egg mixture over vegetables in skillet; stir gently to mix. Cook 3 minutes or until eggs are set around edge, lifting edge to allow uncooked portion to flow underneath. Sprinkle with mozzarella and Parmesan.
5. Broil 3 minutes or until eggs are set and cheese is browned. Cut into wedges to serve. Garnish with parsley.

Makes 2 servings

Baked Cheddar, Broccoli and Mushroom Omelet

- **1 tablespoon butter**
- **1 package (8 ounces) sliced white or cremini mushrooms**
- **1½ cups small broccoli florets (½-inch pieces)**
- **6 eggs**
- **⅓ cup milk**
- **¼ teaspoon salt**
- **¼ teaspoon dried thyme**
- **⅛ teaspoon ground red pepper**
- **½ cup finely chopped green onions**
- **1 cup (4 ounces) shredded sharp Cheddar cheese, divided**

1. Preheat oven to 350°F. Spray 9-inch deep-dish pie plate with nonstick cooking spray.
2. Melt butter in large nonstick skillet over medium-high heat. Add mushrooms and broccoli; cook and stir 6 to 8 minutes or until mushrooms are soft and broccoli is crisp-tender. Transfer to prepared pie plate.
3. Whisk eggs, milk, salt, thyme and red pepper in medium bowl until well blended. Stir in green onions and ¾ cup cheese. Pour evenly over vegetable mixture. Bake 25 to 30 minutes or until knife inserted in center comes out clean.
4. Remove from oven. Sprinkle evenly with remaining ¼ cup cheese; let stand 10 minutes. Cut into wedges to serve.

Makes 6 servings

Mushroom Kale Egg Bites

- **6 eggs**
- **1 cup cottage cheese**
- **¼ cup (1 ounce) shredded Monterey Jack cheese**
- **¼ cup (1 ounce) shredded Swiss cheese**
- **1 teaspoon cornstarch**
- **½ teaspoon white vinegar**
- **½ teaspoon garlic powder**
- **½ teaspoon hot pepper sauce**
- **¼ teaspoon salt**
- **¼ teaspoon black pepper**
- **½ cup finely chopped cremini mushrooms**
- **½ cup finely chopped kale (1 to 2 leaves)**

1. Preheat oven to 300°F. Generously spray 12 standard (2¼-inch) muffin cups with nonstick cooking spray.
2. Combine eggs, cottage cheese, Monterey Jack, Swiss cheese, cornstarch, vinegar, garlic powder, hot pepper sauce, salt and pepper in blender or food processor; blend until smooth. Combine mushrooms and kale in small bowl; mix well.
3. Pour egg mixture evenly into prepared muffin cups; top with vegetable mixture (about 1 tablespoon per cup).
4. Bake 25 to 27 minutes or until set and toothpick inserted into centers comes out with a few moist crumbs. (Egg bites will puff up during baking and sink while cooling.) Cool in pan on wire rack 5 minutes. Loosen edges with small knife or spatula; remove to plate. Serve warm or at room temperature.

Makes 12 egg bites

Wild Rice and Pepper Frittata

- **1 tablespoon olive oil**
- **1 large shallot, minced**
- **1 clove garlic, minced**
- **1 cup chopped fresh shiitake mushroom caps**
- **2 jarred roasted red peppers, chopped**
- **1 cup cooked wild rice***
- **½ teaspoon salt, divided**
- **¼ teaspoon black pepper, divided**
- **⅛ teaspoon paprika**
- **6 eggs**
- **¼ cup shredded Asiago cheese**

If you don't want to use wild rice, use any cooked grain. Quinoa, brown rice, farro or white rice will all work.

1. Preheat broiler. Heat oil in large nonstick ovenproof skillet over medium heat. Add shallot and garlic; cook and stir 1 minute. Add mushrooms; cook and stir 5 minutes or until tender. Stir in red peppers, wild rice, ¼ teaspoon salt, ⅛ teaspoon black pepper and paprika; cook and stir 1 minute or until liquid evaporates. Remove from heat.
2. Whisk eggs, remaining ¼ teaspoon salt and ⅛ teaspoon black pepper in large bowl. Pour eggs into skillet; tilt to spread over rice mixture. Cook over medium heat until eggs are set but still glossy, lifting edge to allow uncooked portion of egg to flow underneath. Sprinkle with cheese.
3. Broil 5 inches from heat source 3 to 4 minutes or until cheese melts and edge is browned. Let stand 2 to 3 minutes. Cut into wedges to serve.

Makes 6 servings

Garden Omelet

- **3 teaspoons butter, divided**
- **⅓ cup chopped onion**
- **⅓ cup chopped red bell pepper**
- **½ cup sliced white or cremini mushrooms**
- **½ teaspoon dried basil**
- **4 eggs**
- **1 tablespoon milk**
- **¼ teaspoon salt**
- **¼ teaspoon black pepper**
- **½ cup (2 ounces) shredded Swiss cheese**

1. Melt 1 teaspoon butter in large nonstick skillet over medium heat. Add onion and bell pepper; cook and stir 2 to 3 minutes or until onion is softened. Add mushrooms and basil; cook and stir 3 to 5 minutes or until mushrooms are tender. Remove from skillet; keep warm.
2. Whisk eggs, milk, salt and black pepper in medium bowl. Melt remaining 2 teaspoons butter in same skillet over medium heat; tilt skillet to coat bottom. Pour egg mixture into skillet; cook until eggs are firm but still moist in center, lifting edge to allow uncooked portion of egg to flow underneath.
3. Spoon vegetable mixture over half of omelet. Sprinkle with cheese. Loosen omelet with spatula and fold in half. Transfer to plate; cut in half to serve.

Makes 2 servings

Overnight Cheesy Vegetable Strata

- **1 cup chopped cremini mushrooms**
- **1 tablespoon olive oil**
- **2 cups coarsely chopped broccoli**
- **½ cup sliced green onions**
- **5 cups whole grain bread cubes**
- **1¼ cups (5 ounces) shredded Swiss cheese, divided**
- **8 eggs**
- **2 cups milk**
- **1 tablespoon Dijon mustard**
- **½ teaspoon salt**
- **½ teaspoon black pepper**

1. Spray 13×9 baking dish with nonstick cooking spray.
2. Heat medium skillet over medium-high heat. Add mushrooms; cook and stir 5 to 7 minutes or until browned. Add oil and broccoli; cook and stir 8 minutes or until broccoli is crisp-tender. Stir in green onions.
3. Layer bread and vegetables in prepared baking dish. Sprinkle ¾ cup cheese evenly over vegetables.
4. Whisk eggs, milk, mustard, salt and pepper in medium bowl. Pour over ingredients in baking dish. Cover and refrigerate overnight.
5. Preheat oven to 350°F. Uncover strata and let stand at room temperature while oven preheats.
6. Bake 30 minutes. Sprinkle remaining ½ cup cheese evenly over top. Bake 10 to 12 minutes or until knife inserted into center comes out clean. Let stand 10 minutes. Cut into squares to serve.

Makes 10 servings

Appetizers & Snacks

Classic Stuffed Mushrooms

1 slice whole wheat bread
16 whole white or cremini mushrooms
½ cup sliced celery
½ cup sliced onion
1 clove garlic
1 teaspoon vegetable oil
1 teaspoon Worcestershire or soy sauce
½ teaspoon dried marjoram
⅛ teaspoon ground red pepper
Salt and black pepper
Dash paprika

1. Preheat oven to 350°F. Tear bread into pieces; place in food processor. Process 30 seconds or until crumbs are formed. Transfer to small bowl; set aside.
2. Remove stems from mushrooms; reserve caps. Place mushroom stems, celery, onion and garlic in food processor; pulse until vegetables are finely chopped.
3. Heat oil in large skillet over medium heat. Add vegetable mixture; cook and stir 5 minutes. Remove from heat. Stir in bread crumbs, Worcestershire sauce, marjoram and red pepper. Season to taste with salt and pepper.
4. Fill mushroom caps evenly with stuffing mixture, pressing down firmly. Place about ½ inch apart in 13×9-inch baking pan. Spray tops with nonstick cooking spray. Sprinkle with paprika.
5. Bake 15 minutes or until heated through.

Makes 8 servings

Note: Mushrooms can be stuffed up to 1 day ahead. Cover and refrigerate filled mushroom caps until ready to serve. Bake in preheated 300°F oven 20 minutes or until heated through.

Vietnamese Vegetarian Spring Rolls

- **12 dried mushrooms (1 ounce)**
- **1 large carrot, cut into julienne strips**
- **2 teaspoons sugar, divided**
- **Hoisin Peanut Sauce (page 29)**
- **3 cups plus 2 tablespoons vegetable oil, divided**
- **1 medium yellow onion, sliced**
- **1 clove garlic, minced**
- **1 tablespoon soy sauce**
- **1 teaspoon toasted sesame oil**
- **1½ cups fresh bean sprouts (4 ounces), rinsed and drained**
- **14 (7-inch) egg roll wrappers**
- **1 egg, beaten**

1. Place mushrooms in small bowl; cover with hot water. Let stand 30 minutes. Combine carrot and 1 teaspoon sugar in another small bowl. Let stand 15 minutes, stirring occasionally.
2. Meanwhile, prepare Hoisin Peanut Sauce.
3. Drain mushrooms, reserving ½ cup liquid. Remove stems and thinly slice caps.
4. Heat wok over medium-high heat 1 minute. Drizzle 2 tablespoons vegetable oil into wok and heat 30 seconds. Add onion; stir-fry 1 minute. Stir in mushrooms, garlic and reserved mushroom liquid. Reduce heat to medium; cover and cook 3 minutes or until mushrooms are tender. Uncover; add soy sauce, sesame oil and remaining 1 teaspoon sugar. Stir-fry 3 to 5 minutes or until all liquid has evaporated. Transfer to medium bowl; cool slightly. Stir in carrot and beans sprouts.
5. Place one wrapper on work surface with corner at bottom, keeping remaining wrappers covered with plastic wrap. Drain mushroom mixture; place 3 tablespoons mixture on bottom third of wrapper. Brush edges of wrapper with some beaten egg.
6. Fold bottom corner of wrapper up over filling. Fold in and overlap the opposite right and left corners to form 3½-inch-wide log; roll up filling to remaining corner. Place on baking sheet; cover with plastic wrap. Repeat with remaining wrappers and filling.
7. Heat remaining 3 cups vegetable oil in wok over medium-high heat to 375°F; adjust heat to maintain temperature during cooking. Fry rolls 2 to 3 minutes or until golden brown, turning once. Drain on paper towels. Serve with sauce.

Makes 14 rolls

Hoisin Peanut Sauce

- **2 tablespoons creamy peanut butter**
- **2 tablespoons water**
- **1 tablespoon soy sauce**
- **⅓ cup hoisin sauce**
- **½ teaspoon toasted sesame oil**
- **1 clove garlic, minced**
- **Dash hot pepper sauce**

Combine peanut butter, water and soy sauce in small bowl; stir until smooth. Stir in hoisin sauce, sesame oil, garlic and hot pepper sauce.

Makes about ½ cup

Breaded Mushrooms

- ½ cup mayonnaise
- 2 teaspoons minced garlic
- 1 teaspoon lemon juice
- ½ cup all-purpose flour
- ½ cup garlic and herb bread crumbs
- ½ cup grated Parmesan cheese
- ½ teaspoon paprika
- ½ teaspoon salt
- ¼ teaspoon black pepper
- 2 eggs
- 1 teaspoon water
- 1 package (8 ounces) whole white or cremini mushrooms

1. Preheat oven to 375°F. Line baking sheet with parchment paper.
2. Stir mayonnaise, garlic and lemon juice in small bowl until well blended. Refrigerate until ready to serve.
3. Whisk flour, bread crumbs, Parmesan cheese, paprika, salt and pepper in shallow bowl. Whisk eggs and water in another shallow bowl.
4. Working with one at a time, dip mushrooms into egg mixture, allowing excess to drip back into bowl. Roll in bread crumb mixture to coat; place on prepared baking sheet.
5. Bake 10 minutes or until golden brown. Serve with garlic mayonnaise for dipping.

Makes 4 servings

Antipasto with Marinated Mushrooms

- **3 tablespoons lemon juice**
- **2 tablespoons chopped fresh parsley**
- **1 clove garlic, minced**
- **½ teaspoon salt**
- **¼ teaspoon dried tarragon**
- **¼ teaspoon black pepper, divided**
- **¾ cup extra virgin olive oil, divided**
- **1 package (8 ounces) white or cremini mushrooms, stems removed**
- **4 teaspoons red wine vinegar**
- **½ teaspoon dried basil**
- **½ teaspoon dried oregano**
- **4 ounces mozzarella cheese, cut into ½-inch cubes**
- **4 ounces prosciutto or ham, thinly sliced**
- **4 ounces provolone cheese, cut into 2-inch sticks**
- **1 jar (10 ounces) pepperoncini peppers, drained**
- **8 ounces hard salami, thinly sliced**
- **1 jar (12 to 14 ounces) marinated artichoke hearts, drained**
- **6 ounces black olives**

1. For mushrooms, combine lemon juice, parsley, garlic, salt, tarragon and ⅛ teaspoon pepper in medium bowl. Add ½ cup oil; whisk until well blended. Add mushrooms; stir to coat. Cover and marinate in refrigerator 4 hours or overnight, stirring occasionally. Drain mushrooms.
2. Combine vinegar, dried basil, oregano and remaining ⅛ teaspoon black pepper in medium bowl. Add remaining ¼ cup oil; whisk until well blended. Add mozzarella cubes; stir to coat. Cover and marinate in refrigerator at least 2 hours. Drain mozzarella.
3. Wrap 1 prosciutto slice around each provolone stick; place on serving plate. Add mozzarella cubes, mushrooms, pepperoncini, salami, artichoke hearts and olives. Garnish with fresh basil.

Makes 6 to 8 servings

Tip: Save the marinades from the mushrooms and the cheese to use as dressings for leafy green salads or pasta salads, or use it to marinate other foods like tofu, chicken or pork.

Wing-Style Mushrooms

2 teaspoons garlic powder
1½ teaspoons paprika
1½ teaspoons poultry seasoning
1½ teaspoons celery seed
1 teaspoon onion powder
½ teaspoon dried sage
½ teaspoon dried thyme
½ teaspoon chili powder
½ teaspoon salt
¼ teaspoon black pepper
1 cup panko bread crumbs
½ cup all-purpose flour
1 cup buttermilk
1 tablespoon hot pepper sauce
2 cups oyster mushroom pieces (about 2 inches)
Blue cheese or ranch dressing
Celery and carrot sticks (optional)

1. Preheat oven to 375°F. Line baking sheet with parchment paper.
2. Whisk garlic powder, paprika, poultry seasoning, celery seed, onion powder, sage, thyme, chili powder, salt and pepper in large bowl; stir in panko. Place flour in medium bowl; slowly whisk in buttermilk until smooth. Stir in hot pepper sauce.
3. Working with one at a time, dip mushrooms in buttermilk mixture; roll in panko mixture to coat. Place on prepared baking sheet.
4. Bake 12 to 15 minutes or until breading is crisp and browned. Serve with blue cheese dressing and vegetable sticks, if desired.

Makes 4 servings

Frittata Stuffed Mushrooms

- 2 tablespoons olive oil, divided
- ½ teaspoon salt
- ½ teaspoon black pepper, divided
- 1 pound cremini or white mushrooms (about 30), stems removed
- ½ cup chopped onion
- 1 teaspoon minced garlic
- ½ (10-ounce) package frozen chopped spinach, thawed and squeezed dry
- ¾ teaspoon dried oregano
- ½ cup plus 2 tablespoons shredded Parmesan cheese, divided
- 1 tablespoon plain dry bread crumbs
- 2 eggs
- ⅓ cup half-and-half

1. Preheat oven to 400°F. Spray 13×9-inch baking pan with nonstick cooking spray.
2. Combine 1 tablespoon oil, salt and ¼ teaspoon pepper in medium bowl; mix well. Add mushroom caps; toss to coat. Place mushrooms cap sides down in prepared baking pan.
3. Heat remaining 1 tablespoon oil in large skillet over medium heat. Add onion, garlic and remaining ¼ teaspoon pepper; cook and stir 5 minutes. Add spinach and oregano; cook and stir until heated through. Remove from heat; stir in ½ cup cheese and bread crumbs. Cool 15 minutes.
4. Whisk eggs and half-and-half in medium bowl until well blended. Stir in spinach mixture. Spoon filling into mushrooms. Sprinkle with remaining 2 tablespoons cheese. Bake 10 to 15 minutes or until mushrooms are tender and filling is set. Serve warm or at room temperature.

Makes 30 mushrooms

Veggie Pepper Pizza Poppers

- **6 mini sweet bell peppers (red, orange and yellow)**
- **½ cup marinara sauce**
- **½ cup (2 ounces) shredded mozzarella cheese**
- **¼ cup chopped white mushrooms**
- **Sliced black olives**
- **1 teaspoon chopped fresh oregano**

1. Preheat oven to 350°F. Line baking sheet with parchment paper.
2. Cut peppers in half horizontally. Remove seeds but keep stems intact. Spoon marinara sauce into pepper halves; top with cheese, mushrooms and olives. Sprinkle with oregano.
3. Bake 10 minutes or until cheese is melted and begins to brown.

Makes 12 poppers

Creamy Mushroom Cups

- **2 tablespoons butter**
- **4 ounces white mushrooms, coarsely chopped**
- **¼ teaspoon salt**
- **2 cloves garlic, minced**
- **¼ cup whipping cream**
- **2 tablespoons dry sherry**
- **15 frozen mini phyllo shells, thawed and warmed according to package directions**
- **¼ cup chopped fresh parsley**

1. Melt butter in large nonstick skillet over medium heat. Add mushrooms and salt; cook and stir 3 minutes or until tender. Add garlic; cook and stir 15 seconds.
2. Stir in cream and sherry; cook and stir 2 minutes or until thickened.
3. Divide mushroom mixture evenly among phyllo shells. Sprinkle with parsley; serve immediately.

Makes 15 cups

Pesto Turkey Stuffed Mushrooms

- **1 pound cremini mushrooms (about 30)**
- **½ pound ground turkey**
- **¼ cup panko bread crumbs**
- **¼ cup plus 1 tablespoon shredded Parmesan cheese, divided**
- **¼ cup pesto sauce**
- **¼ teaspoon salt**
- **Chopped fresh parsley (optional)**

1. Preheat oven to 400°F. Spray 13×9-inch baking pan with nonstick cooking spray. Remove stems from mushrooms; place cap side down in prepared pan.
2. Combine turkey, panko, ¼ cup cheese, pesto and salt in medium bowl; mix well. Shape mixture by teaspoonfuls into balls; press into mushrooms. Sprinkle remaining 1 tablespoon cheese over stuffed mushrooms.
3. Bake about 20 minutes or until filling is cooked through (165°F). Transfer mushrooms to serving plate; cool slightly. Garnish with parsley.

Makes 30 mushrooms

Beer-Battered Mushrooms

- **1 cup all-purpose flour**
- **½ teaspoon baking powder**
- **½ teaspoon chili powder**
- **¼ teaspoon salt, plus additional for seasoning**
- **⅛ teaspoon black pepper**
- **1 cup beer**
- **1 egg, separated**
- **Vegetable oil for frying**
- **1 pound white or cremini mushrooms**

1. Combine flour, baking powder, chili powder, ¼ teaspoon salt and pepper in medium bowl. Whisk beer and egg yolk in another medium bowl.
2. Beat egg white in large bowl with electric mixer at high speed until soft peaks form.
3. Stir beer mixture into flour mixture just until blended. Fold in egg white.
4. Heat 2 inches of oil in large saucepan over medium-high heat to 365°F; adjust heat to maintain temperature during cooking.
5. Working in batches, dip mushrooms in batter. Add to oil; cook 1 to 2 minutes or until golden brown, turning occasionally. Drain on paper towels; immediately season with additional salt.

Makes 6 to 8 servings

Smoky Bacon Mushroom Toasts

- **1 package (12 ounces) bacon, chopped**
- **1 onion, diced**
- **1 red bell pepper, diced**
- **1 pound white or cremini mushrooms, diced**
- **Salt and black pepper**
- **24 (½-inch) toasted French bread slices**
- **Chopped fresh parsley**

1. Cook bacon in large skillet over medium heat until crisp. Remove with slotted spoon to paper towels to drain. Discard all but 2 tablespoons drippings from skillet.
2. Add onion and bell pepper to skillet; cook and stir over medium-high heat 2 minutes or until vegetables begin to soften. Add mushrooms; season with salt and black pepper. Cook and stir 8 to 10 minutes or until mushroom liquid is almost evaporated. Cool 5 minutes.
3. Spread mushroom mixture on bread slices. Sprinkle with bacon and parsley.

Makes 24 appetizers

Garlic Mushrooms

- 1 pound white or cremini mushrooms
- 2 tablespoons olive oil
- 1 teaspoon garlic powder
- 1 teaspoon Italian seasoning
- ½ teaspoon salt
- ¼ teaspoon black pepper
- Chopped fresh parsley
- Ranch dressing

1. Preheat oven to 375°F. Cut mushrooms in half.
2. Combine mushrooms, oil, garlic powder, Italian seasoning, salt and pepper in large bowl; toss to coat. Spread on baking sheet.
3. Bake 15 minutes until tender and browned, stirring once. Sprinkle with parsley. Serve with ranch dressing for dipping.

Makes 4 servings

SOUPS & STEWS

Hearty Beefy Beer Soup

- 1 tablespoon vegetable oil
- 12 ounces boneless beef round steak, cut into ½-inch pieces
- 1 large onion, chopped
- 2 medium carrots, sliced
- 2 stalks celery, chopped
- 5 cups beef broth
- 1 bottle (12 ounces) stout or dark ale
- ¾ teaspoon dried oregano
- ½ teaspoon salt
- ⅛ teaspoon black pepper
- 1 can (about 15 ounces) kidney beans, rinsed and drained
- 1 small zucchini, cut into ½-inch pieces
- 4 ounces white mushrooms, sliced

1. Heat oil in large saucepan or Dutch oven over medium heat. Add beef, onion, carrots and celery; cook and stir 6 minutes or until beef is no longer pink and carrots and celery are crisp-tender.
2. Stir in broth, stout, oregano, salt and pepper; bring to a boil over high heat. Reduce heat to medium-low; simmer, uncovered, 45 minutes or until beef is fork-tender.
3. Stir in beans, zucchini and mushrooms; bring to a boil over high heat. Reduce heat to medium-low; simmer, uncovered, 5 minutes or until zucchini is tender.

Makes 6 servings

Mixed Mushroom Soup

- **6 tablespoons butter, divided**
- **1 small onion, finely chopped**
- **4 cups vegetable broth, divided**
- **8 ounces assorted fresh mushrooms, such as cèpes, shiitake, oyster, portobello, cremini, morels or chanterelles *or* 8 ounces white mushrooms, sliced**
- **1 teaspoon lemon juice**
- **¼ cup all-purpose flour**
- **¼ teaspoon white pepper**
- **1 cup half-and-half or whipping cream**
- **Fresh chives (optional)**

1. Melt 2 tablespoons butter in large saucepan over medium-high heat. Add onion; cook and stir 3 minutes or until softened. Stir in 3½ cups broth; cover and bring to a boil over high heat. Reduce heat to medium-low.
2. Meanwhile, slice stems and caps of shiitake, chanterelle or morel mushrooms; add to broth mixture. Thinly slice stems of cèpes, oyster, portobello or cremini mushrooms; reserve caps. Add to broth mixture; simmer 10 minutes.
3. Slice reserved mushroom caps. Melt 2 tablespoons butter in medium skillet over medium-high heat. Add mushroom caps; cook and stir just until softened. Transfer to soup with slotted spoon.
4. Add remaining 2 tablespoons butter and lemon juice to same skillet; stir until butter is melted. Stir in flour and pepper until smooth. Whisk in remaining ½ cup broth until smooth. Add to soup; cook until soup thickens, stirring constantly. Stir in half-and-half; cook until heated through. Garnish with chives.

Makes 4 servings

Beef Barley Stew

- 2 pounds boneless beef chuck roast, trimmed and cut into ¾-inch pieces
- 2½ teaspoons salt, divided
- ½ teaspoon black pepper
- 2 tablespoons vegetable oil
- 1 package (16 ounces) baby carrots
- 1 onion, finely chopped
- 1 package (16 ounces) white or cremini mushrooms, thickly sliced
- 2 cloves garlic, minced
- 1 teaspoon dried thyme
- 1 teaspoon dried marjoram
- 4 cups beef broth
- 1 can (about 14 ounces) diced tomatoes
- 1 cup water
- 2 bay leaves
- 1 cup uncooked pearl barley
- 1 cup frozen peas

1. Season beef with 1 teaspoon salt and pepper. Heat oil in Dutch oven over medium-high heat. Add half of beef; cook 4 to 5 minutes or until browned, turning occasionally. Remove to plate; repeat with remaining beef.

2. Add carrots and onion to Dutch oven; cook 5 minutes or until onion is softened, stirring to scrape up browned bits. Add mushrooms; cook about 8 minutes or until liquid is released and almost evaporated, stirring occasionally. Add garlic, thyme and marjoram; cook and stir 1 minute. Stir in beef, broth, tomatoes, water, bay leaves and remaining 1½ teaspoons salt; bring to a boil. Reduce heat to low; cover and simmer 1 hour 15 minutes.

3. Stir in barley; cover and simmer 45 minutes. Stir in peas; cook, uncovered, 10 minutes or until barley is tender and peas are heated through. Remove bay leaves; season with additional salt and pepper, if desired.

Makes 8 servings

Turkey and Veggie Soup

- **2 tablespoons butter**
- **1 package (8 ounces) sliced white or cremini mushrooms**
- **½ cup chopped onion**
- **1 red bell pepper, chopped**
- **½ cup thinly sliced celery**
- **1 carrot, thinly sliced**
- **¾ teaspoon salt**
- **½ teaspoon dried thyme**
- **4 cups chicken or turkey broth**
- **2 cups chopped cooked turkey**
- **4 ounces uncooked egg noodles**
- **1 cup half-and-half**
- **½ cup frozen peas**

1. Melt butter in large saucepan or Dutch oven over medium-high heat. Add mushrooms and onion; cook and stir 5 minutes or until onion is translucent.
2. Add bell pepper, celery, carrot, salt and thyme; cook and stir 10 minutes or until vegetables are softened. Add broth; bring to a boil. Stir in turkey and noodles. Reduce heat to medium-low; simmer 15 minutes or until noodles are tender.
3. Stir in half-and-half and peas; cook until soup is heated through.

Makes 4 to 6 servings

Double Mushroom Soup

- 1 package (1 ounce) dried shiitake mushrooms
- 2 teaspoons vegetable oil
- 1 large onion, chopped
- 2 cloves garlic, minced
- 2 cups sliced white mushrooms
- 2 cans (about 14 ounces each) vegetable broth
- 2 ounces cooked ham, cut into thin slivers (optional)
- ½ cup thinly sliced green onions
- 1 tablespoon dry sherry
- 1 tablespoon soy sauce
- 1 tablespoon cornstarch

1. Place shiitake mushrooms in small bowl; cover with boiling water. Let stand 20 minutes to soften. Drain mushrooms and rinse well; squeeze out excess water. Cut off and discard stems; slice caps.
2. Heat oil in large saucepan over medium heat. Add onion and garlic; cook and stir 5 minutes or until softened. Stir in shiitake and white mushrooms; cook 4 minutes, stirring occasionally.
3. Stir in broth; bring to a boil over high heat. Reduce heat to medium; cover and simmer 15 minutes.
4. Stir in ham, if desired, and green onions; cook until heated through. Stir sherry and soy sauce into cornstarch in small bowl until smooth. Add to soup; cook 2 minutes or until thickened, stirring occasionally.

Makes 6 servings

Gingery Beef Noodle Soup

- 2 tablespoons soy sauce
- 1 tablespoon minced fresh ginger
- ¼ teaspoon red pepper flakes
- 1 boneless beef top sirloin steak (about 12 ounces)
- 1 tablespoon peanut or vegetable oil
- 2 cups sliced white or cremini mushrooms
- 2 cans (about 14 ounces each) beef broth
- 1 cup (3 ounces) fresh snow peas, cut diagonally into 1-inch pieces
- 1½ cups hot cooked lo mein noodles (2 ounces uncooked)
- 1 green onion, cut diagonally into thin slices
- 1 teaspoon toasted sesame oil
- Red bell pepper strips (optional)

1. Combine soy sauce, ginger and red pepper flakes in small bowl; mix well. Pour over steak in shallow dish; turn to coat. Marinate at room temperature 15 minutes.
2. Heat peanut oil in deep skillet or wok over medium-high heat. Drain steak, reserving marinade. Add steak to skillet; cook 5 minutes per side or until desired doneness. Remove to cutting board; let stand 10 minutes.
3. Add mushrooms to skillet; stir-fry 2 minutes. Add broth, snow peas and reserved marinade; bring to a boil, stirring to scrape up browned bits. Reduce heat to medium-low; stir in noodles.
4. Cut steak lengthwise in half, then cut crosswise into thin slices. Stir into soup; cook just until heated through. Stir in green onion and sesame oil. Garnish with bell pepper strips.

Makes 4 servings

Cream of Mushroom Soup

- ½ cup dried porcini mushrooms (about ½ ounce)
- 1 tablespoon olive oil
- 2 cups chopped onions
- 1 package (8 ounces) sliced cremini or white mushrooms
- 2 cloves garlic, minced
- ¼ teaspoon dried thyme
- ¼ cup all-purpose flour
- 4 cups vegetable broth
- ½ cup whipping cream
- ⅓ cup Marsala wine (optional)
- Salt and black pepper

1. Place porcini mushrooms in small bowl; cover with boiling water. Let stand 15 minutes or until tender.
2. Meanwhile, heat oil in large saucepan over medium heat. Add onions; cook and stir 5 minutes or until softened, stirring occasionally. Add cremini mushrooms, garlic and thyme; cook 8 minutes, stirring occasionally. Add flour; cook and stir 1 minute. Stir in broth.
3. Drain porcini mushrooms, reserving liquid. Chop mushrooms; add to saucepan with reserved liquid. Bring to a boil. Reduce heat to medium-low; simmer 10 minutes. Cool slightly. If desired, remove some of cremini mushrooms for garnish.
4. Working in batches, process soup in food processor or blender until smooth (or use handheld immersion blender). Return to saucepan over medium-low heat. Stir in cream and Marsala, if desired; season with salt and pepper. Simmer 5 minutes or until heated through. Garnish with reserved mushrooms.

Makes 4 servings

Turkey Vegetable Rice Soup

- **1½ pounds turkey drumsticks (2 small)**
- **1 teaspoon salt**
- **8 cups cold water**
- **1 medium onion, cut into quarters**
- **2 tablespoons soy sauce**
- **¼ teaspoon black pepper**
- **1 bay leaf**
- **2 carrots, sliced**
- **⅓ cup uncooked rice**
- **4 ounces white mushrooms, sliced**
- **1 cup fresh snow peas, cut in half crosswise**
- **1 cup coarsely chopped bok choy**

1. Place turkey in large saucepan or Dutch oven; season with salt. Add water, onion, soy sauce, pepper and bay leaf; bring to a boil over high heat. Reduce heat to medium-low; simmer, uncovered, 1½ hours or until turkey is tender.
2. Remove turkey to plate; set aside until cool enough to handle. Let broth cool slightly; skim fat. Remove and discard bay leaf. Remove turkey meat from bones; discard skin and bones. Cut turkey into bite-size pieces.
3. Add carrots and rice to broth in saucepan; bring to a boil over high heat. Reduce heat to medium-low; cook 10 minutes.
4. Add mushrooms and turkey to soup; bring to a boil over high heat. Reduce heat to medium-low; cook 5 minutes. Add snow peas and bok choy; bring to a boil over high heat. Reduce heat to medium-low; cook 8 minutes or until rice and vegetables are tender.

Makes 6 servings

Navy Bean Vegetable Soup

- 1 cup dried navy beans, rinsed and sorted
- 3 cups water
- 1½ teaspoons salt, divided
- 6 cups vegetable broth
- 1 pound leeks (about 2), cut into ½-inch pieces
- 12 ounces new potatoes or small red potatoes
- 2 cups sliced white mushrooms
- 1½ cups thinly sliced carrots
- 1½ teaspoons dried thyme
- 1 bay leaf
- ½ teaspoon black pepper
- 1 package (3½ ounces) crispy tortilla strips
- Chopped tomatoes

1. Combine beans and 3 cups water in large saucepan; bring to a boil over high heat. Remove from heat; cover and let stand 30 minutes.

2. Return beans and water to a boil over high heat. Reduce heat to low; simmer, covered, 30 minutes. Stir in ½ teaspoon salt; cover and simmer 1 hour or until beans are tender; drain.

3. Add broth, leeks, potatoes, mushrooms, carrots, thyme, bay leaf, remaining 1 teaspoon salt and pepper to Dutch oven. Bring to a boil over high heat. Reduce heat to low; cover and simmer 25 minutes. Add beans; cook 5 minutes. Remove and discard bay leaf. Ladle soup into shallow bowls; top with tortilla strips and tomatoes.

Makes 8 servings

Lentil and Portobello Soup

- 8 ounces portobello mushrooms
- 1 tablespoon olive oil
- 1 onion, chopped
- 2 carrots, cut into ½-inch-thick rounds
- 2 cloves garlic, minced
- 1 can (28 ounces) diced tomatoes
- 1 can (about 14 ounces) vegetable broth
- 1 cup dried lentils, rinsed and sorted
- 1 teaspoon salt
- 1 teaspoon dried rosemary
- 1 bay leaf

1. If mushrooms have stems, remove and coarsely chop. Cut caps in half, then cut into ½-inch pieces.

2. Heat oil in large saucepan over medium-high heat. Add onion, carrots and garlic; cook and stir 5 minutes or until onion is softened. Stir in tomatoes, broth, lentils, mushroom caps and stems, salt, rosemary and bay leaf. Reduce heat to medium-low; cover and simmer 30 minutes or until lentils are tender. Remove and discard bay leaf.

Makes 6 servings

Chicken Rotini Soup

- 2 tablespoons butter
- 8 ounces boneless skinless chicken breasts, cut into ½-inch pieces
- 1 medium onion, chopped
- 4 ounces white mushrooms, sliced
- ½ teaspoon salt
- ¼ teaspoon black pepper
- ¼ teaspoon dried tarragon
- 4 cups chicken broth
- 1 teaspoon Worcestershire sauce
- 1 cup uncooked rotini pasta
- 1 zucchini, thinly sliced

1. Melt butter in Dutch oven or large saucepan over medium heat. Add chicken, onion, mushrooms, salt, pepper and tarragon; cook and stir 5 minutes or until onion is softened and chicken is lightly browned.
2. Stir in broth and Worcestershire sauce. Bring to a boil over high heat. Stir in pasta. Reduce heat to medium-low; simmer 5 minutes. Add zucchini; simmer 5 minutes or until pasta is tender.

Makes 4 servings

SANDWICHES & PIZZAS

Easy Mushroom Pizza

- **3 to 3½ cups all-purpose flour**
- **1¼ cups warm water (120°F)**
- **3 tablespoons olive oil, divided**
- **1 package (¼ ounce) instant yeast**
- **1¼ teaspoons salt, divided**
- **8 to 10 white or cremini mushrooms, cut into ⅛-inch-thick slices**
- **⅛ teaspoon black pepper**
- **1 cup pizza sauce, divided**
- **3 cups (12 ounces) shredded mozzarella cheese, divided**
- **Pinch dried oregano and red pepper flakes**
- **Fresh thyme or chopped fresh basil (optional)**

1. Combine 3 cups flour, water, 2 tablespoons oil, yeast and 1 teaspoon salt in large bowl of stand mixer. Mix with dough hook at low speed about 2 minutes or until soft dough forms, adding additional flour 1 tablespoon at a time if necessary to clean side of bowl. Knead at medium-low speed 5 minutes.
2. Shape dough into a ball. Place dough in greased bowl; turn to grease top. Cover and let rise in warm place about 1 hour or until doubled in size.
3. Preheat oven to 500°F. Combine mushrooms, 1 teaspoon oil, remaining ¼ teaspoon salt and pepper in small bowl; toss to coat.
4. Turn out dough onto lightly floured surface. Divide dough in half; roll each half into 12-inch circle on lightly floured surface. Place dough on pizza pans or baking sheets.
5. Brush edges of dough with remaining 2 teaspoons oil. Spread ½ cup sauce over each crust, leaving ¼-inch border. Sprinkle with 1½ cups cheese; top with mushrooms. Sprinkle with oregano and red pepper flakes.
6. Bake about 10 minutes or until crust is golden brown and cheese is melted. Sprinkle with fresh thyme, if desired. Cool on wire rack 5 minutes; cut into wedges to serve.

Makes 8 servings (2 pizzas)

Mushroom Po' Boys

Rèmoulade Sauce (recipe follows)*
1 cup buttermilk
1 tablespoon hot pepper sauce
1¼ cups all-purpose flour
1 teaspoon salt
1 teaspoon smoked paprika
¼ teaspoon onion powder
¼ teaspoon black pepper
1 package (4 ounces) sliced shiitake mushrooms
1 package (3 ounces) oyster mushrooms, cut into 2-inch or bite-size pieces
Vegetable oil for frying
1 loaf French bread, ends trimmed, cut into 4 pieces and split
Sliced fresh tomatoes and finely shredded iceberg lettuce

****Or substitute plain mayonnaise for serving.***

1. Prepare Rèmoulade Sauce; cover and refrigerate until ready to use.
2. Combine buttermilk and hot pepper sauce in medium bowl. Whisk flour, salt, paprika, onion powder and black pepper in another medium bowl. Dip mushroom pieces, a few at a time, in buttermilk mixture; roll in flour mixture to coat. Dip again in buttermilk mixture and roll in flour mixture; place on plate. Repeat with remaining mushrooms.
3. Heat 2 inches of oil in large saucepan over medium-high heat to 360°F; adjust heat to maintain temperature during cooking. Working in batches, cook mushrooms 2 to 3 minutes or until golden brown. Drain on paper towels.
4. Serve mushrooms on French bread with tomatoes, lettuce and Rèmoulade sauce.

Makes 4 servings

Rèmoulade Sauce: Combine ½ cup mayonnaise, 2 tablespoons Dijon or coarse-grain mustard, 1 tablespoon lemon juice, 1 clove garlic, minced, and ½ teaspoon hot pepper sauce in small bowl.

Veggie Pizza

- ¾ to 1 cup all-purpose flour, divided
- ½ cup whole wheat flour
- 1 teaspoon instant yeast
- 1½ teaspoons dried basil, divided
- ¼ teaspoon salt
- ½ cup very warm water (120° to 130°F)
- 1 tablespoon olive oil
- 1 clove garlic, minced
- 1 teaspoon yellow cornmeal
- ½ cup tomato sauce
- 1 cup thinly sliced white or cremini mushrooms
- ¾ cup sliced jarred roasted red peppers
- ½ cup thinly sliced zucchini
- ⅓ cup chopped green onions
- 1 cup (4 ounces) shredded mozzarella cheese
- ¼ teaspoon red pepper flakes

1. Combine ¾ cup all-purpose flour, whole wheat flour, yeast, 1 teaspoon basil and salt in large bowl. Stir in water, oil and garlic until soft, slightly sticky dough forms. Knead dough on lightly floured surface about 5 minutes, adding remaining ¼ cup all-purpose flour as needed to make smooth and elastic dough. Shape dough into a ball. Cover; let rest 10 minutes.
2. Preheat oven to 400°F. Spray 12-inch pizza pan or baking sheet with nonstick cooking spray; sprinkle with cornmeal. Roll dough into large circle on lightly floured surface. Transfer to prepared pan, stretching dough to edge of pan. (Too much rolling makes crust heavy and dense; stretching dough to fit pan is best.)
3. Combine tomato sauce and remaining ½ teaspoon basil in small bowl; spread evenly over crust. Top with mushrooms, roasted pepper, zucchini, green onions and mozzarella; sprinkle with red pepper flakes. Bake 20 to 25 minutes or until crust is golden brown and cheese is melted.

Makes 4 servings

Mushroom Cheesesteak Sandwiches

- **1 package (8 ounces) sliced white mushrooms**
- **1½ teaspoons salt, divided**
- **2 tablespoons vegetable oil, divided**
- **1 medium onion, cut into ½-inch slices**
- **1 green bell pepper, cut into ½-inch slices**
- **½ teaspoon garlic powder**
- **½ teaspoon black pepper, divided**
- **1 pound skirt or flank steak**
- **4 French bread or hoagie rolls, split and toasted**
- **8 slices provolone cheese**

1. Place mushrooms in dry large skillet; add ¾ teaspoon salt and cook over medium-high heat about 5 minutes or until mushrooms release their liquid and begin to brown, stirring occasionally. Add 1 tablespoon oil, onion, bell pepper and ¼ teaspoon black pepper to skillet; cook 6 to 8 minutes or until onion and bell pepper begin to brown, stirring occasionally. Remove vegetables to medium bowl; cover to keep warm.

2. Cut steak in half lengthwise, then cut crosswise (against the grain) into ¼-inch slices. Season with remaining ¾ teaspoon salt and ¼ teaspoon black pepper.

3. Heat remaining 1 tablespoon oil in same skillet over medium-high heat. Add steak in single layer; cook 1 to 2 minutes per side or just until edges are browned. Add steak and any juices in skillet to vegetables in bowl; stir to blend.

4. Spoon one fourth of steak and vegetable mixture on bottom of each roll; top with two slices of cheese. Cover sandwiches loosely with foil and let stand briefly to melt cheese.

Makes 4 servings

Kale and Mushroom Pizza

- **1 package (13.8 ounces) refrigerated pizza dough**
- **1 tablespoon olive oil**
- **1 cup chopped onion**
- **1 package (8 ounces) sliced white or cremini mushrooms**
- **3 cloves garlic, minced**
- **4 cups packed coarsely chopped kale**
- **¼ teaspoon red pepper flakes**
- **½ cup pizza sauce**
- **1 cup (4 ounces) finely shredded mozzarella cheese**

1. Preheat oven to 425°F. Spray 15×10-inch baking sheet with nonstick cooking spray. Unroll pizza dough on prepared pan. Press dough evenly into pan and ½ inch up sides. Prick dough all over with fork. Bake 7 to 10 minutes or until lightly browned.
2. Heat oil in large nonstick skillet over medium heat. Add onion; cook and stir 10 minutes or until lightly browned. Add mushrooms and garlic; cook and stir 4 minutes. Add kale and red pepper flakes; cover and cook 5 minutes to wilt kale. Uncover; cook and stir 3 to 4 minutes or until vegetables are tender.
3. Spread pizza sauce over crust. Spread kale mixture evenly over sauce; top with cheese. Bake 10 minutes or until crust is golden brown. Cut into squares to serve.

Makes 4 servings

Mushroom Tofu Burgers

- **7 ounces extra firm tofu**
- **3 teaspoons olive oil, divided**
- **1 package (8 ounces) cremini mushrooms, coarsely chopped**
- **½ medium onion, coarsely chopped**
- **1 clove garlic, minced**
- **1 cup old-fashioned oats**
- **⅓ cup finely chopped walnuts**
- **1 egg**
- **½ teaspoon salt**
- **½ teaspoon onion powder**
- **¼ teaspoon dried thyme**
- **6 English muffins or hamburger buns, split and toasted**
- **Lettuce, tomato and red onion slices (optional)**

1. Crumble tofu and spread on small baking sheet or freezer-safe plate. Freeze 1 hour or until firm.
2. Heat 1 teaspoon oil in large nonstick skillet over medium heat. Add mushrooms, onion and garlic; cook and stir 10 minutes or until mushrooms are tender and liquid has evaporated. Remove from heat; cool slightly.
3. Combine mushroom mixture, tofu, oats, walnuts, egg, salt, onion powder and thyme in food processor or blender; process until combined. (Some tofu pieces may remain). Shape mixture into six ⅓-cup patties.
4. Heat 1 teaspoon oil in same skillet over medium-low heat. Working in batches, cook patties 5 minutes per side or until firm and lightly browned. Repeat with remaining oil and patties. Serve on English muffins with lettuce, tomato and red onion, if desired.

Makes 6 servings

Cheesy Mushroom Melt

4 French rolls
4 slices Swiss cheese
4 slices Cheddar cheese
4 slices provolone cheese
2 cups sliced white mushrooms
1 avocado, thinly sliced
1 cup thinly sliced iceberg lettuce
½ cup thinly sliced yellow or white onion
2 plum tomatoes, thinly sliced
2 dill pickles, thinly sliced lengthwise
Optional toppings: mayonnaise, mustard, vinaigrette, sliced banana peppers and/or giardiniera

1. Preheat oven to 400°F. Line baking sheet with foil. Split sides and long ends of rolls, leaving one long end attached. Place rolls cut sides down on prepared baking sheet. Bake 5 minutes.

2. Remove baking sheet from oven; turn rolls over. For each sandwich, cut one slice of each cheese in half diagonally; arrange cheese halves on each half of roll, overlapping to fit. Top each bottom half of roll with ½ cup mushrooms.

3. Bake 5 to 7 minutes until cheese is melted and bread is toasted.

4. Layer avocado, lettuce, onion, tomatoes, pickles and desired toppings over mushrooms. Close sandwiches and press gently; cut in half to serve.

Makes 4 servings

Mushroom and Goat Cheese Pizza

- 1 package (13.8 ounces) refrigerated pizza dough
- 2 tablespoons olive oil
- 1 red onion, thinly sliced
- 3 cloves garlic, minced
- 1 package (8 ounces) sliced white mushrooms
- 1 package (6 ounces) sliced cremini mushrooms
- 1 package (5 ounces) sliced shiitake mushrooms
- Salt and black pepper
- 1 package (4 ounces) goat cheese, softened
- 2 cups (8 ounces) shredded mozzarella cheese or pizza cheese blend, divided
- ¾ cup sun-dried tomatoes (not packed in oil), finely chopped

1. Preheat oven to 425°F. Spray 15×10-inch baking sheet with nonstick cooking spray. Unroll pizza dough on prepared pan. Press dough evenly into pan and ½ inch up sides. Prick dough all over with fork. Bake 7 to 10 minutes or until lightly browned.
2. Meanwhile, heat oil in large skillet over medium-high heat. Add onion; cook and stir 5 minutes. Add garlic; cook and stir 30 seconds. Add white and cremini mushrooms; cook 5 minutes, stirring occasionally. Add shiitake mushrooms; season with salt and pepper. Cook and stir 10 minutes or until liquid has evaporated.
3. Spread goat cheese on pizza crust. Sprinkle with 1½ cups mozzarella cheese and tomatoes. Top with mushroom mixture. Sprinkle with remaining ½ cup mozzarella cheese.
4. Bake 10 to 12 minutes or until cheese is melted and crust is golden brown. Cut into squares to serve.

Makes 4 servings

Beet and Walnut Burgers

- 6 tablespoons boiling water
- 2 tablespoons ground flaxseed
- 3 tablespoons olive oil, divided
- 1 onion, chopped
- 1 package (8 ounces) sliced white or cremini mushrooms
- 3 cloves garlic, chopped
- 2 teaspoons salt
- 1 teaspoon dried thyme
- ½ teaspoon smoked paprika
- ½ teaspoon ground cumin
- ¼ teaspoon black pepper
- ½ cup old-fashioned oats
- 1½ cups toasted walnuts
- 1 large beet (about 1 pound), peeled and grated on large holes of box grater
- 1 can (about 15 ounces) cannellini beans, rinsed and drained
- 1 tablespoon soy sauce
- Hamburger buns or rolls
- Optional toppings: mixed greens, pickles, sliced jalapeño peppers, sliced avocado, sliced red onion and/or sliced tomatoes

1. Combine boiling water and flaxseed in small bowl; mix well. Set aside until completely cool.
2. Heat 1 tablespoon oil in large skillet over medium-high heat. Add onion, mushrooms and garlic; cook and stir 8 minutes or until vegetables are softened and mushrooms are browned. Remove from heat; stir in salt, thyme, paprika, cumin and pepper. Cool slightly.
3. Place oats in food processor or blender; process until finely ground. Add walnuts; pulse until nuts are coarsely chopped. Transfer oats and walnuts to large bowl. Place mushroom mixture and beet in food processor; pulse until finely chopped. Add beans; pulse just until blended, leaving beans chunky. Add to bowl with nuts. Add flaxseed mixture and soy sauce; mix well. Refrigerate at least 30 minutes.
4. Heat 1 tablespoon oil in large skillet over medium-high heat. Shape mixture by heaping ½ cupfuls into ½-inch patties; place in skillet. Cook 5 minutes per side or until well browned and heated through. Repeat with remaining beet mixture, adding additional oil as needed. Serve on buns with desired toppings.

Makes 8 servings

MAIN DISHES

Ginger Tofu Bowl

- **7 tablespoons soy sauce, divided**
- **2 teaspoons minced fresh ginger**
- **1 teaspoon toasted sesame oil**
- **1 package (about 14 ounces) firm tofu, drained and cut into ½-inch cubes**
- **1 cup uncooked brown rice**
- **½ seedless cucumber, thinly sliced**
- **¼ teaspoon salt**
- **¼ teaspoon sugar**
- **¼ cup rice vinegar**
- **1 package (8 ounces) sliced cremini or white mushrooms**
- **1 cup thawed frozen shelled edamame**
- **2 carrots, julienned or thinly sliced**
- **4 green onions, thinly sliced**
- **Pickled ginger and sesame seeds**

1. Combine 6 tablespoons soy sauce, fresh ginger and sesame oil in large shallow bowl. Add tofu; stir to coat. Cover and refrigerate 2 hours or overnight.
2. Prepare rice according to package directions.
3. Meanwhile, place cucumbers in shallow bowl. Sprinkle with salt and sugar; toss to coat. Add vinegar; mix well.
4. Heat medium skillet over medium heat. Add mushrooms; cook and stir 5 minutes or until tender and lightly browned. Remove from heat; stir in remaining 1 tablespoon soy sauce.
5. Divide rice among four bowls. Arrange tofu, mushrooms, cucumbers, edamame and carrots over rice; top with green onions, pickled ginger and sesame seeds.

Makes 4 servings

Chicken Croustade

- 1½ pounds boneless skinless chicken breasts, chopped into ¼-inch pieces
- Salt and black pepper
- 2 tablespoons canola oil
- 1 large portobello mushroom cap
- 1 shallot, minced
- ¼ cup white wine
- ¼ cup chicken broth
- 1 tablespoon chopped fresh thyme
- ¼ teaspoon paprika
- ¼ teaspoon ground cumin
- 1 package puff pastry shells
- 1 egg yolk
- 2 tablespoons whipping cream
- 3 tablespoons grated Parmesan cheese
- Minced and whole chives (optional)

1. Season chicken all over with salt and pepper. Heat oil in large skillet over medium-high heat. Add chicken; cook 4 minutes without stirring, then cook and stir until browned on all sides. Transfer to bowl.
2. Meanwhile, scrape gills from mushroom cap with spoon and discard. Chop mushroom cap into ¼-inch pieces.
3. Heat same skillet over medium heat. Add shallot; cook 2 minutes or until softened. Add wine, stirring to scrape up browned bits; cook until wine is reduced to about 2 tablespoons. Return chicken to skillet; add mushroom, broth, thyme, paprika and cumin. Season with additional salt and pepper. Reduce heat to medium-low; cover and simmer 30 minutes.
4. Meanwhile, bake puff pastry shells according to package directions and cool completely.
5. Whisk egg yolk and cream in small bowl. Stir 1 tablespoon hot cooking liquid into egg mixture; stir mixture back into sauce in skillet. Cook and stir 10 to 15 minutes or until thickened. Stir in Parmesan. Divide chicken filling among puff pastry shells. Garnish with chives.

Makes 6 to 8 servings

Tofu Satay with Peanut Sauce

Satay

- 1 package (about 14 ounces) firm tofu, drained and pressed*
- 1/3 cup water
- 1/3 cup soy sauce
- 1 tablespoon toasted sesame oil
- 1 teaspoon minced garlic
- 1 teaspoon minced fresh ginger
- 1 package (8 ounces) white or cremini mushrooms
- 1 red bell pepper, cut into 1-inch pieces

Peanut Sauce

- 1 can (about 13 ounces) unsweetened coconut milk
- 1/2 cup creamy peanut butter
- 2 tablespoons packed brown sugar
- 1 tablespoon rice vinegar
- 1 to 2 teaspoons red Thai curry paste

**Place tofu on paper towels in a colander in the sink. Place a small, flat plate on top of tofu and weigh it down with a large can. Let stand 30 minutes.*

1. Cut tofu into 24 cubes. Combine water, soy sauce, sesame oil, garlic and ginger in small bowl. Place tofu, mushrooms and bell pepper in large resealable food storage bag. Add soy sauce mixture; seal bag and turn gently to coat. Marinate 30 minutes, turning occasionally. Soak eight 8-inch bamboo skewers in water 20 minutes.
2. Preheat oven to 400°F. Spray 13×9-inch glass baking dish with nonstick cooking spray.
3. Drain tofu mixture; discard marinade. Thread tofu, mushrooms and bell pepper onto skewers. Place skewers in prepared baking dish.
4. Bake 25 minutes or until tofu cubes are lightly browned and vegetables are softened.
5. Meanwhile, whisk coconut milk, peanut butter, brown sugar, vinegar and curry paste in small saucepan over medium heat. Bring to a boil, stirring constantly. Reduce heat to low; cook 20 minutes or until creamy and thick, stirring frequently. Serve skewers with sauce.

Makes 4 servings

Turkey and Roasted Vegetable Bowl

- **1 head cauliflower, cut into florets**
- **1 head broccoli, cut into florets**
- **3 tablespoons olive oil, divided**
- **1¼ teaspoons salt, divided**
- **⅛ teaspoon black pepper**
- **1 sweet potato, peeled and cubed**
- **1 package (8 ounces) whole white or cremini mushrooms, stemmed and sliced**
- **⅓ cup dried lentils**
- **⅓ cup tricolor or white quinoa**
- **¼ cup tahini**
- **1 teaspoon lemon juice**
- **¼ teaspoon ground cumin**
- **6 tablespoons cold water**
- **1 tablespoon minced fresh cilantro or parsley**
- **1 slice (¼-inch-thick) deli turkey *or* 1 cup cubed cooked turkey or chicken**
- **¾ cup shredded red and/or green cabbage or coleslaw mix**

1. Preheat oven to 400°F. Combine cauliflower and broccoli in large bowl. Drizzle with 2 tablespoons oil and sprinkle with ½ teaspoon salt and ⅛ teaspoon pepper; toss to coat. Spread mixture on one side of large baking sheet. Place sweet potatoes on other side of baking sheet. Drizzle with ½ tablespoon oil and season with ¼ teaspoon salt; toss to coat. Bake 30 minutes or until vegetables are tender, stirring once.
2. Meanwhile, place mushrooms on small baking sheet; drizzle with remaining ½ tablespoon oil and sprinkle with ¼ teaspoon salt. Bake 20 minutes or until dry and dark brown.
3. Bring medium saucepan of salted water to a boil. Add lentils; cook 5 minutes. Add quinoa. Reduce heat to medium; cook about 15 minutes or until quinoa and lentils are tender. Drain and return to saucepan.
4. For sauce, whisk tahini, lemon juice, cumin and remaining ¼ teaspoon salt in medium bowl. Whisk in enough cold water until sauce is smooth and desired consistency. Stir in cilantro.
5. Cut turkey into cubes. Divide lentil mixture among three bowls. Arrange cauliflower, broccoli, sweet potato and cabbage around lentils. Top with turkey, mushrooms and sauce.

Makes 3 servings

Steak and Mushroom Pie

- **3 tablespoons butter, divided**
- **1½ pounds boneless beef chuck steak, cut into 1-inch cubes**
- **2 medium onions, chopped**
- **3 stalks celery, cut into ½-inch slices**
- **1 package (8 ounces) sliced white or cremini mushrooms**
- **½ teaspoon dried thyme**
- **½ cup dry red wine**
- **¼ cup all-purpose flour**
- **1 cup beef broth**
- **2 tablespoons tomato paste**
- **1 tablespoon Dijon mustard**
- **½ teaspoon salt**
- **¼ teaspoon black pepper**
- **1 refrigerated pie crust (half of 15-ounce package)**
- **1 egg, lightly beaten**

1. Spray 9- or 10-inch deep-dish pie plate or 1½-quart baking dish with nonstick cooking spray. Melt 2 tablespoons butter in large saucepan over medium-high heat. Add half of beef; cook 4 to 5 minutes or until browned, turning occasionally. Remove to plate; repeat with remaining beef.
2. Melt remaining 1 tablespoon butter in same saucepan over medium-high heat. Add onions, celery, mushrooms and thyme; cook and stir 4 to 5 minutes or until vegetables begin to soften. Add wine; cook and stir 3 to 4 minutes or until almost evaporated. Add flour; cook and stir 1 minute. Stir in broth, tomato paste, mustard and beef; bring to a boil. Reduce heat to medium-low; cover and simmer 1 hour to 1 hour 10 minutes or until beef is very tender, stirring occasionally. Remove from heat; stir in salt and pepper. Pour into prepared pie plate; let cool 20 minutes.
3. Preheat oven to 400°F. Roll out pie crust on lightly floured surface to fit top of pie plate. Place crust over filling; decoratively flute or crimp edges. Brush crust with egg; cut several small slits in top of crust with tip of knife.
4. Bake 23 to 25 minutes or until crust is golden brown. Let stand 5 minutes before serving.

Makes 4 to 6 servings

Chicken Madeira

- 4 boneless skinless chicken breasts (about 6 ounces each)
- ½ teaspoon salt
- ¼ teaspoon black pepper
- 3 tablespoons butter, divided
- 1 tablespoon olive oil
- 1 package (8 ounces) sliced white or cremini mushrooms
- 1½ cups Madeira wine
- 1½ cups beef broth
- 8 ounces fresh asparagus, trimmed
- ¼ cup plus 1 tablespoon water, divided
- 1 tablespoon cornstarch
- 4 slices mozzarella cheese

1. Pound chicken to ¼-inch thickness between two pieces of waxed paper or plastic wrap with meat mallet or rolling pin. Season with salt and pepper.
2. Heat 1 tablespoon butter and oil in large skillet over medium heat. Add chicken; cook 4 to 5 minutes per side or until lightly browned. Transfer to plate; tent with foil. Add 1 tablespoon butter and mushrooms to skillet; cook 8 minutes or until mushrooms are browned and liquid has evaporated, stirring to scrape up browned bits. Remove mushrooms to medium bowl.
3. Add Madeira and broth to skillet; bring to a boil over high heat. Reduce heat to medium; cook 10 to 12 minutes or until reduced by half.
4. Meanwhile, preheat broiler. Place asparagus in medium microwavable dish with ¼ cup water; cover with vented plastic wrap. Microwave on HIGH 4 minutes or until crisp-tender.
5. Stir remaining 1 tablespoon water into cornstarch in small bowl until smooth. Whisk into reduced liquid in skillet; cook and stir 2 minutes or until thickened. Add remaining 1 tablespoon butter; stir until melted. Stir in cooked mushrooms.
6. Place chicken on medium baking sheet; top with cheese and asparagus. Broil 2 minutes or until cheese is melted. Remove chicken to serving plates; top with sauce.

Makes 4 servings

Vegetable Enchiladas

- **1 tablespoon vegetable oil**
- **2 large poblano peppers or green bell peppers, cut into 2-inch strips**
- **1 large zucchini, cut into 2-inch strips**
- **1 large red onion, sliced**
- **1 cup sliced white or cremini mushrooms**
- **1 teaspoon ground cumin**
- **1 pound fresh tomatillos (about 8 large), peeled**
- **1 small jalapeño pepper, minced**
- **1 clove garlic**
- **½ teaspoon salt**
- **1 cup loosely packed fresh cilantro**
- **12 corn tortillas, warmed**
- **2 cups (8 ounces) shredded Mexican cheese blend, divided**

1. Preheat oven to 400°F.
2. Heat oil in large nonstick skillet over medium heat. Add poblano peppers, zucchini, onion, mushrooms and cumin; cook 8 to 10 minutes or until vegetables are crisp-tender, stirring occasionally.
3. Meanwhile, place tomatillos in large microwavable bowl. Cover with vented plastic wrap; microwave on HIGH 6 to 7 minutes or until very tender.
4. Combine tomatillos with juice, jalapeño, garlic and salt in food processor or blender; process until smooth. Add 1 cup cilantro; pulse until combined and cilantro is coarsely chopped.
5. Divide vegetables evenly among tortillas. Spoon heaping tablespoon of cheese in center of each tortilla; roll up to enclose filling. Place in 13×9-inch baking dish. Pour sauce over enchiladas; sprinkle with remaining 1 cup cheese.
6. Cover and bake 18 to 20 minutes or until cheese is melted and enchiladas are heated through.

Makes 6 servings

Cranberry Smothered Chicken

- **4 boneless skinless chicken breasts (about 6 ounces each)**
- **1 teaspoon salt**
- **½ teaspoon black pepper**
- **½ cup all-purpose flour**
- **¼ cup vegetable oil**
- **3 cloves garlic, minced**
- **½ cup chicken broth**
- **2 tablespoons butter**
- **3 medium onions, coarsely chopped**
- **2 green bell peppers, cut into thin strips**
- **10 white or cremini mushrooms, sliced**
- **1 can (16 ounces) whole berry cranberry sauce**
- **1 cup orange juice**
- **½ cup raspberry or balsamic vinegar**
- **1 tablespoon water**
- **1 tablespoon Worcestershire sauce**
- **1 tablespoon cornstarch**

1. Season chicken all over with salt and black pepper. Place flour in medium bowl; add chicken and turn to coat.
2. Heat oil in large skillet over medium-high heat. Add chicken; cook about 5 minutes per side or until chicken is browned. Drain drippings from skillet. Add garlic; cook 30 seconds. Add broth; bring to a boil over high heat. Reduce heat to low; cover and simmer 30 minutes.
3. Melt butter in another large skillet over medium-high heat. Add onions, bell peppers and mushrooms; cook and stir 10 minutes or until vegetables are softened. Stir in cranberry sauce, orange juice and vinegar. Reduce heat to medium; cook and stir about 5 minutes or until cranberry sauce melts and mixture is heated through.
4. Stir water and Worcestershire sauce into cornstarch in small bowl until smooth; add to sauce and vegetables in skillet. Cook and stir over low heat until thickened. Season with additional salt and black pepper.
5. Place chicken on serving plates; top with sauce.

Makes 4 servings

Trout with Mushrooms and Potato-Parsnip Mash

- 4 medium potatoes, peeled and cut into chunks
- 4 medium parsnips, peeled and cut into chunks
- 4 tablespoons butter, divided
- Salt and black pepper
- ¼ cup all-purpose flour
- ½ teaspoon dried thyme
- ¼ teaspoon salt
- ¼ teaspoon black pepper
- 2 fresh whole trout (about 12 ounces each), filleted
- 12 ounces cremini mushrooms, sliced
- ¼ cup dry white or rosé wine

1. Combine potatoes and parsnips in large saucepan; add cold water to cover. Bring to a boil over high heat. Reduce heat to medium-low; simmer until vegetables are fork-tender. Drain and return to saucepan; mash until desired consistency. Stir in 2 tablespoons butter; season with salt and pepper. Keep warm.
2. Meanwhile, combine flour, thyme, ¼ teaspoon salt and ¼ teaspoon pepper in shallow dish. Coat fillets with flour mixture; shake off excess. Melt remaining 2 tablespoons butter in large skillet over medium-high heat. Add fish to skillet in single layer; cook 1 to 2 minutes per side or until fish begins to flake when tested with fork. Remove to plate; keep warm.
3. Add mushrooms to skillet; cook and stir 5 minutes or until softened. Season with salt and pepper. Add wine; cook and stir until most of liquid has evaporated.
4. Serve fish over mashed vegetables; top with mushrooms.

Makes 4 servings

Bacon-Wrapped Chicken with Mushrooms and Onions

- **4 boneless skinless chicken breasts (about 6 ounces each)**
- **Salt and black pepper**
- **8 slices turkey bacon or regular bacon**
- **2 tablespoons olive oil, divided**
- **1 package (8 ounces) cremini mushrooms, stems trimmed, thinly sliced**
- **1 medium onion, thinly sliced**
- **¼ cup sherry**
- **¼ cup chicken broth**
- **½ teaspoon salt**
- **¼ teaspoon black pepper**

1. Preheat oven to 350°F. Spray 13×9-inch baking pan with nonstick cooking spray.
2. Season chicken with salt and pepper; wrap two bacon slices around each chicken breast. Heat 1 tablespoon oil in large nonstick skillet over medium-high heat. Add chicken; cook 3 minutes per side or until chicken and bacon are browned. Transfer to prepared baking pan. Bake about 45 minutes or until chicken is cooked through (165°F).
3. Heat remaining 1 tablespoon oil in medium skillet over medium-high heat. Add mushrooms and onion; cook and stir about 5 minutes or until tender. Add sherry; cook and stir until absorbed. Add broth; cook and stir until reduced slightly. Stir in ½ teaspoon salt and ¼ teaspoon pepper.
4. Place chicken on serving plates; serve with mushroom mixture.

Makes 4 servings

Vegetable Primavera Crêpes

- **2 teaspoons vegetable oil**
- **1 cup chopped onion**
- **1 pound thin fresh asparagus, trimmed and cut into ½-inch pieces**
- **1 package (8 ounces) sliced cremini mushrooms**
- **1 red bell pepper, chopped**
- **2 ounces cream cheese, cubed**
- **½ teaspoon salt**
- **½ teaspoon black pepper**
- **4 tablespoons grated Parmesan cheese, divided**
- **5 tablespoons sliced fresh basil, divided**
- **8 (9-inch) prepared French crêpes***

Look for packages of prepared crêpes in the produce section of the supermarket.

1. Heat oil in large skillet over medium heat. Add onion; cook and stir 3 minutes. Add asparagus, mushrooms and bell pepper; cook and stir 8 to 10 minutes or until vegetables are tender.
2. Add cream cheese, salt and black pepper; cook until cream cheese is melted, stirring constantly. Remove from heat; stir in 3 tablespoons Parmesan cheese and 3 tablespoons basil.
3. Spoon ½ cup mixture down center of each crêpe; roll up to enclose filling. Top crêpes evenly with remaining 1 tablespoon Parmesan cheese and 2 tablespoons basil. Serve immediately.

Makes 8 crêpes

Mushroom Ragoût with Polenta

- **1 package (about ½ ounce) dried porcini mushrooms**
- **½ cup boiling water**
- **1 can (about 14 ounces) vegetable broth**
- **½ cup yellow cornmeal**
- **1 teaspoon salt, divided**
- **1 tablespoon olive oil**
- **⅓ cup sliced shallots or chopped onion**
- **1 package (4 ounces) sliced mixed fresh exotic mushrooms or sliced cremini mushrooms**
- **4 cloves garlic, minced**
- **1 can (about 14 ounces) Italian-style diced tomatoes**
- **¼ teaspoon red pepper flakes**
- **¼ cup chopped fresh basil or parsley**

1. Place porcini mushrooms in small bowl; add boiling water. Let stand 10 minutes.
2. Meanwhile, whisk together broth, cornmeal and ½ teaspoon salt in large microwavable bowl. Cover with waxed paper; microwave on HIGH 5 minutes. Whisk well; microwave on HIGH 3 to 4 minutes or until polenta is very thick. Whisk again; cover and set aside.
3. Heat oil in large nonstick skillet over medium-high heat. Add shallots; cook and stir 3 minutes. Add fresh mushrooms and garlic; cook and stir 3 to 4 minutes. Stir in tomatoes, red pepper flakes and remaining ½ teaspoon salt.
4. Drain porcini mushrooms, reserving liquid. Strain liquid and add to skillet. If mushrooms are large, cut into ½-inch pieces; add to skillet. Bring to a boil over high heat. Reduce heat to low; cook 5 minutes or until slightly thickened. Stir in basil.
5. Spoon polenta onto four plates; top with mushroom mixture.

Makes 4 servings

Nut Roast

- 1½ cups unsalted walnuts, pecans, almonds or cashews
- 2 tablespoons olive oil
- 1 onion, finely chopped
- 4 ounces cremini mushrooms (about 6 large), sliced
- 2 cloves garlic, minced
- 1 can (about 14 ounces) diced tomatoes
- 1 cup old-fashioned oats
- 2 eggs, lightly beaten
- 2 tablespoons all-purpose flour
- 1 tablespoon chopped fresh sage
- 1 tablespoon chopped fresh parsley
- 1 teaspoon chopped fresh thyme
- 1 teaspoon salt
- ¼ teaspoon black pepper

1. Preheat oven to 350°F. Spray 8×4-inch loaf pan with nonstick cooking spray. Place nuts in food processor. Pulse until finely chopped, allowing some larger pieces to remain. Transfer to large bowl.
2. Heat oil in medium skillet over medium heat. Add onion, mushrooms and garlic; cook and stir 3 minutes or until softened. Transfer mixture to bowl with nuts.
3. Stir in tomatoes, oats, eggs, flour, sage, parsley, thyme, salt and pepper until combined. Spoon mixture into prepared pan. Bake 45 to 50 minutes or until firm and browned. Cool slightly before slicing.

Makes 6 to 8 servings

Sirloin with Mushrooms and Whiskey-Cream Sauce

- **1 package (8 ounces) sliced cremini mushrooms**
- **1½ pounds sirloin steak**
- **½ teaspoon salt**
- **¼ teaspoon black pepper**
- **2 tablespoons butter**
- **1 tablespoon vegetable oil**
- **½ cup Irish whiskey**
- **½ cup whipping cream**
- **½ cup beef broth**
- **Chopped fresh chives**

1. Heat large skillet over medium-high heat. Add mushrooms; cook 8 minutes or until liquid evaporates, stirring occasionally. Transfer to bowl.
2. Sprinkle both sides of steak with salt and pepper. Heat butter and oil in same skillet over medium-high heat. Add steak; cook about 3 minutes per side or to desired doneness. Remove to plate; keep warm.
3. Add whiskey to skillet; cook 2 minutes, stirring to scrape up browned bits. Add cream and broth; cook and stir 3 minutes. Stir in any accumulated juices from steak.
4. Return mushrooms to skillet; cook and stir 2 minutes or until sauce thickens. Slice steak; serve with mushroom sauce. Sprinkle with chives.

Makes 4 servings

PASTA & NOODLES

Creamy Mushroom Stroganoff

- **3 tablespoons butter**
- **2 medium onions, sliced**
- **2½ pounds white or cremini mushrooms, thickly sliced**
- **1 teaspoon dried thyme**
- **¾ teaspoon salt**
- **½ teaspoon black pepper**
- **6 garlic cloves, minced**
- **⅓ cup dry white wine**
- **1 cup vegetable broth**
- **2 teaspoons vegetarian Worcestershire sauce or soy sauce**
- **2 teaspoons Dijon mustard**
- **8 ounces extra wide egg noodles**
- **⅔ cup sour cream**
- **2 tablespoons chopped fresh parsley**

1. Melt butter in Dutch oven or large saucepan over medium-high heat. Add onions, mushrooms, thyme, ½ teaspoon salt and ¼ teaspoon pepper; cook and stir 15 minutes or until mushrooms are tender and liquid has almost completely evaporated. Add garlic; cook 2 minutes. Pour in wine; cook and stir 1 minute. Stir in broth, Worcestershire sauce and mustard. Reduce heat to medium-low; cover and simmer 30 minutes.

2. Cook pasta in large saucepan of salted boiling water according to package directions for al dente. Drain and return to saucepan.

3. Remove mushroom mixture from heat. Stir 3 tablespoons cooking liquid into sour cream in medium bowl. Stir mixture back into saucepan. Stir in parsley and remaining ¼ teaspoon salt and ¼ teaspoon pepper. Divide noodles evenly among four plates; top with mushroom mixture.

Makes 4 servings

Capellini Primavera

- ¼ cup (½ stick) butter
- 1 cup chopped onion
- 1 cup julienned or shredded carrots
- 4 cups (1-inch) broccoli florets (2 small heads)
- 1 package (8 ounces) sliced white or cremini mushrooms
- 1 yellow squash, halved lengthwise and thinly sliced (about 2 cups)
- 2 teaspoons minced garlic
- 1 teaspoon salt
- 1 can (14 ounces) crushed tomatoes
- ½ cup drained oil-packed sun-dried tomatoes, finely chopped
- 1 tablespoon finely chopped fresh parsley
- ½ teaspoon dried oregano
- ½ teaspoon dried rosemary
- ⅛ teaspoon red pepper flakes
- 12 ounces uncooked angel hair pasta (capellini)
- 2 tablespoons olive oil
- Black pepper

1. Melt butter in large skillet over medium-high heat. Add onion and carrots; cook and stir 3 minutes or until onion is softened. Add broccoli, mushrooms, squash, garlic and salt; cook 10 minutes or until mushrooms are tender, stirring frequently.

2. Reduce heat to medium-low. Add crushed tomatoes, sun-dried tomatoes, parsley, oregano, rosemary and red pepper flakes; cook 10 minutes, stirring occasionally.

3. Meanwhile, cook pasta in large saucepan of salted boiling water according to package directions for al dente. Drain and place in large bowl, reserving ½ cup pasta cooking water.

4. Stir reserved pasta cooking water into sauce; add sauce to pasta and toss to coat. Drizzle with oil; stir gently to coat. Season with additional salt and black pepper.

Makes 6 servings

Chicken Scaloppine with Mushrooms and Artichokes

- ½ cup all-purpose flour
- ½ teaspoon salt
- ¼ teaspoon black pepper
- 4 boneless skinless chicken breasts (about 6 ounces each)
- 5 tablespoons butter, divided
- 1 tablespoon olive oil
- 1 package (3 to 4 ounces) diced pancetta *or* ⅓ cup diced prosciutto
- 1 pound sliced white or cremini mushrooms
- 1 can (14 ounces) artichoke hearts, drained and sliced
- 3 tablespoons capers, rinsed and drained
- ⅓ cup lemon juice
- 3 tablespoons white wine
- ¾ cup whipping cream
- ¾ cup chicken broth
- 2 teaspoons cornstarch
- 1 package (16 ounces) angel hair pasta (capellini), cooked and drained
- Chopped fresh parsley (optional)

1. Preheat oven to 250°F. Line baking sheet with foil. Combine flour, salt and pepper in shallow dish. Pound chicken to ⅛-inch thickness between sheets of waxed paper or plastic wrap with meat mallet or rolling pin. Cut each chicken breast in half crosswise. Coat both sides of chicken with flour mixture, shaking off excess.

2. Heat 1 tablespoon butter and oil in large skillet over medium-high heat. Add chicken in single layer; cook about 3 minutes per side or until golden brown and cooked through (165°F). (Cook chicken in batches, if necessary.) Place on prepared baking sheet; keep warm in oven.

3. Add pancetta to skillet; cook and stir over medium heat 3 minutes or until lightly browned. Add mushrooms; cook about 8 minutes or until mushrooms begin to brown, stirring occasionally. Stir in artichokes and capers; cook 4 minutes, stirring to scrape up browned bits. Keep warm over low heat.

4. Combine lemon juice and wine in small saucepan; bring to a boil over medium-high heat. Boil until reduced by one third. Stir in cream; cook over medium heat 4 minutes or until slightly thickened. Stir broth into cornstarch in small bowl until blended. Add to saucepan; cook and stir 3 minutes or until sauce thickens. Add remaining 4 tablespoons butter, 1 tablespoon at a time, whisking until sauce is smooth and well blended. Add sauce to mushroom mixture; cook and stir until heated through.

5. Divide pasta among four plates; top with chicken and mushroom mixture. Garnish with parsley.

Makes 4 servings

Turkey Veggie Lasagna

- **2 tablespoons olive oil, divided**
- **1 pound ground turkey**
- **2 cups packed chopped stemmed kale**
- **1 onion, chopped, divided**
- **3 cloves garlic, minced, divided**
- **2 teaspoons salt, divided**
- **1 can (28 ounces) crushed tomatoes**
- **1 can (about 15 ounces) tomato sauce**
- **1 teaspoon Italian seasoning**
- **1 package (8 ounces) sliced white or cremini mushrooms**
- **1 medium zucchini, cut in half lengthwise and thinly sliced crosswise**
- **1 container (15 ounces) ricotta cheese**
- **5 cups (20 ounces) shredded Italian cheese blend or mozzarella cheese, divided**
- **½ cup chopped fresh parsley**
- **1 egg**
- **¼ teaspoon black pepper**
- **12 no-boil lasagna noodles**

1. Preheat oven to 350°F. Spray 13×9-inch baking dish with nonstick cooking spray.
2. Heat 1 tablespoon oil in large saucepan over medium-high heat. Add turkey, kale, onion, 2 cloves garlic and 1 teaspoon salt; cook and stir about 5 minutes or until turkey is no longer pink, stirring to break up meat. Stir in tomatoes, tomato sauce and Italian seasoning; cook 10 minutes.
3. Meanwhile, heat remaining 1 tablespoon oil in large skillet over medium-high heat. Add mushrooms, zucchini and ½ teaspoon salt; cook and stir about 5 minutes or until vegetables are tender.
4. Combine ricotta, 1 cup shredded cheese, parsley, egg, remaining 1 clove garlic, ½ teaspoon salt and black pepper in medium bowl; mix well.
5. Spread ¼ cup tomato sauce mixture over bottom of prepared baking dish. Top with three noodles. Spread one third of ricotta mixture over noodles. Top with 1 cup shredded cheese, 1½ cups sauce and three more noodles. Spread one third of ricotta mixture over noodles. Top with vegetables, 1 cup shredded cheese, 1½ cups sauce and three more noodles. Spread remaining ricotta mixture over noodles; top with 1 cup shredded cheese and 1 cup sauce. Top with remaining three noodles and remaining sauce. Sprinkle with remaining 1 cup shredded cheese. Cover loosely with greased foil.
6. Bake 30 minutes. Remove cover; bake 10 minutes or until sauce is bubbly and hot and cheese is melted. Let stand 10 minutes before serving.

Makes 6 to 8 servings

Pesto Cavatappi

Pesto

- 2 cups packed fresh basil leaves*
- 1 cup walnuts, toasted**
- ½ cup shredded Parmesan cheese, plus additional for garnish
- 4 cloves garlic
- 1 teaspoon salt
- ¼ teaspoon black pepper
- ¾ cup olive oil

Pasta

- 1 package (16 ounces) uncooked cavatappi pasta
- 1 tablespoon olive oil
- 2 plum tomatoes, diced (1½ cups)
- 1 package (8 ounces) sliced white mushrooms
- ¼ cup dry white wine
- ¼ cup vegetable broth
- ¼ cup whipping cream

**Or substitute 1 cup packed fresh parsley leaves for half of basil.*

***To toast walnuts, cook in medium skillet over medium heat 4 to 5 minutes or lightly browned, stirring frequently.*

1. For pesto, combine basil, walnuts, ½ cup cheese, garlic, salt and pepper in food processor; pulse until coarsely chopped. With motor running, add ¾ cup oil in thin, steady stream; process until well blended. Measure 1 cup pesto for pasta; reserve remaining pesto for another use.
2. Cook pasta in large saucepan of salted boiling water according to package directions for al dente. Drain and return to saucepan; keep warm.
3. Meanwhile, heat 1 tablespoon oil in large skillet over medium-high heat. Add tomatoes and mushrooms; cook about 7 minutes or until most of liquid has evaporated, stirring occasionally. Add wine, broth and cream; bring to a boil. Reduce heat to low; cook about 4 minutes or until sauce has thickened slightly. Stir in 1 cup pesto; cook just until heated through.
4. Pour sauce over pasta; stir gently to coat. Serve with additional cheese.

Makes 4 to 6 servings

Mushroom Noodle Stir-Fry

8 ounces uncooked Chinese egg noodles or spaghetti
8 ounces shiitake mushrooms, stemmed and thinly sliced (¼-inch slices)
Pinch of salt
2 tablespoons butter
1 tablespoon minced garlic
2 teaspoons honey
½ cup stir-fry sauce
2 to 3 tablespoons water
2 green onions, sliced diagonally
2 tablespoons grated Parmesan cheese

1. Cook noodles according to package directions; drain and rinse under cold water to stop cooking.

2. Heat large skillet over medium-high heat. Add mushrooms; cook and stir about 5 minutes or until browned. Season with salt. Add butter, garlic and honey; cook and stir 1 minute or until butter is melted and garlic is fragrant but not browned.

3. Add stir-fry sauce, 2 tablespoons water and noodles; cook and stir 2 to 3 minutes or until heated through. Add additional water by teaspoonfuls, if necessary, to loosen sauce. Divide noodles between serving bowls; top with green onions and cheese.

Makes 2 main-dish or 4 side-dish servings

Chicken Pesto Pasta

- **8 ounces uncooked bowtie pasta (farfalle)**
- **2 teaspoons olive oil**
- **1 pound boneless skinless chicken breasts, cut into 1-inch pieces**
- **1 teaspoon salt, divided**
- **½ teaspoon black pepper**
- **1 clove garlic, minced**
- **1 package (8 ounces) sliced white mushrooms**
- **3 tablespoons butter**
- **2 tablespoons all-purpose flour**
- **½ teaspoon salt**
- **1 cup milk**
- **¼ cup pesto sauce**
- **½ cup chopped drained oil-packed sun-dried tomatoes**
- **Grated Parmesan cheese**

1. Cook pasta in large saucepan of salted boiling water according to package directions for al dente. Drain and return to saucepan; keep warm.
2. Meanwhile, heat oil in large skillet over medium-high heat. Add chicken, ½ teaspoon salt, pepper and garlic; cook and stir 5 to 7 minutes or until chicken is cooked through (165°F). Add mushrooms; cook and stir 3 to 5 minutes or until mushrooms are tender. Transfer to bowl; keep warm.
3. Melt butter in same skillet over medium-high heat. Reduce heat to low; whisk in flour and salt until well blended. Slowly whisk in milk; cook and stir 2 to 3 minutes until mixture begins to boil. Remove from heat; stir in pesto and sun-dried tomatoes until well blended.
4. Add chicken mixture and pasta to skillet; cook and stir over medium heat until heated through. Serve with Parmesan.

Makes 4 servings

Sukiyaki

- 1 package (3¾ ounces) cellophane noodles (bean threads)
- ½ cup beef broth
- ½ cup teriyaki sauce
- ¼ cup sake, rice wine or dry sherry
- 1 tablespoon sugar
- 1 pound beef tenderloin or top sirloin steaks
- 2 tablespoons vegetable oil, divided
- 6 ounces fresh shiitake mushrooms, stems removed and sliced
- 8 ounces firm tofu, drained and cut into 1-inch cubes
- 6 green onions, cut into 2-inch pieces
- 1 package (10 ounces) baby spinach

1. Place noodles in bowl; cover with water. Let stand 30 minutes or until softened; drain. Cut into 4-inch lengths; set aside.
2. Combine beef broth, teriyaki sauce, sake and sugar in small bowl; set aside. Cut beef crosswise into ¼-inch strips.
3. Heat wok over high heat 1 minute. Drizzle 1 tablespoon oil into wok and heat 30 seconds. Add half of beef; stir-fry 3 minutes or until browned. Transfer to bowl; set aside. Repeat with remaining 1 tablespoon oil and beef.
4. Reduce heat to medium. Add mushrooms to wok; stir-fry 1 minute and move up one side of wok. Add tofu to bottom of wok; fry 1 minute, stirring gently. Move up another side of wok. Add green onions to bottom of wok. Add broth mixture and bring to a boil. Move onions up side of wok.
5. Add noodles and spinach, keeping each in separate piles and stirring gently to soften in teriyaki sauce. Push up side of wok. Add beef and any juices; heat through.

Makes 4 servings

Cheesy Spinach and Mushroom Fettuccine

- **8 ounces uncooked fresh spinach fettuccine or dried fettuccine**
- **1 tablespoon vegetable oil**
- **1½ cups sliced white mushrooms**
- **2 green onions, finely chopped**
- **1 teaspoon garlic, minced**
- **1 package (10 ounces) frozen spinach, thawed and drained***
- **2 tablespoons water**
- **1 container (15 ounces) ricotta cheese**
- **¾ cup whipping cream**
- **1 egg**
- **½ teaspoon salt**
- **½ teaspoon ground nutmeg**
- **½ teaspoon black pepper**
- **½ cup (2 ounces) shredded Swiss cheese**

Or substitute 10 ounces coarsely chopped fresh baby spinach.

1. Preheat oven to 350°F. Spray 1½-quart baking dish with nonstick cooking spray. Cook pasta according to package directions; drain and return to saucepan.
2. Heat oil in medium skillet over medium heat. Add mushrooms, green onions and garlic; cook and stir until mushrooms are softened. Add spinach and water; cover and cook about 3 minutes or until spinach is wilted.
3. Combine ricotta cheese, cream, egg, salt, nutmeg and black pepper in large bowl. Gently stir in noodles and vegetables; toss to coat evenly. Spread noodle mixture in prepared baking dish. Sprinkle with Swiss cheese.
4. Bake 25 to 30 minutes or until knife inserted halfway into center comes out clean.

Makes 4 servings

Vegetable Pasta Sauce

- 1 tablespoon olive oil
- 1½ cups sliced white or cremini mushrooms
- 1 red bell pepper, diced
- 1 green bell pepper, diced
- 1 yellow squash, cut into ¼-inch slices
- 1 zucchini, cut into ¼-inch slices
- 4 green onions, sliced
- 1 can (6 ounces) tomato paste
- 2 tablespoons Italian seasoning
- 1 tablespoon chopped fresh parsley
- 3 cloves garlic, minced
- 1 teaspoon salt
- 1 teaspoon red pepper flakes (optional)
- 1 teaspoon black pepper
- 1 can (28 ounces) diced tomatoes
- 1 can (about 14 ounces) whole tomatoes, undrained
- 1 package (16 ounces) uncooked penne pasta
- Parmesan cheese

1. Heat oil in large saucepan over medium-high heat. Add mushrooms, bell peppers, squash, zucchini and green onions; cook and stir 10 minutes or until vegetables are softened.

2. Add tomato paste, Italian seasoning, parsley, garlic, salt, red pepper flakes, if desired, and black pepper; cook and stir 1 minute. Add tomatoes; mix well. Reduce heat to low; simmer at least 30 minutes, breaking up whole tomatoes with wooden spoon.

3. Cook pasta in large saucepan of salted boiling water according to package directions for al dente. Drain and place in serving bowls. Top with sauce; serve with Parmesan.

Makes 6 servings

Japanese Pan Noodles

- **⅓ cup soy sauce**
- **⅓ cup packed brown sugar**
- **1 tablespoon mirin**
- **1 teaspoon chili garlic sauce**
- **1 tablespoon vegetable or peanut oil**
- **2 cups small broccoli florets (about 2 small crowns or 10 ounces)**
- **2 cups sliced white or cremini mushrooms**
- **1 cup matchstick carrots (about 2 medium) or shredded carrots**
- **1 tablespoon finely chopped fresh ginger**
- **1 package (14 to 16 ounces) cooked udon noodles***
- **Black sesame seeds**
- **Fresh cilantro sprigs (optional)**

Or substitute 1 package (16 ounces) dried or fresh udon noodles; cook and drain according to package directions.

1. Combine soy sauce and brown sugar in small saucepan; bring to a boil over medium-high heat. Reduce heat to medium; cook about 10 minutes or until reduced and thickened slightly, stirring frequently. Remove from heat; stir in mirin and chili garlic sauce until well blended.
2. Heat oil in wok or large saucepan over high heat. Add broccoli and mushrooms; cook and stir about 5 minutes or until vegetables are crisp-tender. Add carrots and ginger; cook and stir 1 minute. Add soy sauce mixture and noodles; cook 3 to 5 minutes or until noodles are heated through and most of sauce is absorbed, stirring frequently.
3. Sprinkle with sesame seeds; garnish with cilantro.

Makes 2 to 4 servings

Lentil Ragù

- **2 tablespoons olive oil**
- **1 onion, chopped**
- **1 carrot, chopped**
- **1 stalk celery, chopped**
- **2 cloves garlic, minced**
- **1 teaspoon salt**
- **½ teaspoon dried oregano**
- **Pinch red pepper flakes**
- **3 tablespoons tomato paste**
- **¼ cup dry white wine**
- **1 can (28 ounces) crushed tomatoes**
- **1 can (about 14 ounces) diced tomatoes**
- **1 cup dried lentils, rinsed and sorted**
- **1 portobello mushroom, gills removed, finely chopped**
- **1½ cups water**
- **1 package (16 ounces) uncooked whole wheat rotini**

1. Heat oil in large saucepan over medium heat. Add onion, carrot and celery; cook and stir 10 minutes or until onion is lightly browned and carrot is softened.
2. Stir in garlic, salt, oregano and red pepper flakes. Add tomato paste; cook and stir 1 minute. Add wine; cook and stir until absorbed. Stir in crushed tomatoes, diced tomatoes, lentils, mushroom and water; bring to a simmer. Reduce heat to medium; partially cover and simmer about 40 minutes or until lentils are tender, removing cover after 20 minutes.
3. Cook pasta in large saucepan of salted boiling water according to package directions for al dente. Drain and stir into sauce.

Makes 6 servings

Soba Stir-Fry

- **8 ounces uncooked soba (buckwheat) noodles**
- **1 tablespoon olive oil**
- **2 cups sliced shiitake mushrooms**
- **1 red bell pepper, thinly sliced**
- **2 whole dried red chiles *or* ¼ teaspoon red pepper flakes**
- **1 clove garlic, minced**
- **2 cups shredded napa cabbage**
- **½ cup vegetable broth**
- **2 tablespoons tamari or soy sauce**
- **1 tablespoon rice wine or dry sherry**
- **2 teaspoons cornstarch**
- **1 package (14 ounces) firm tofu, drained and cut into 1-inch cubes**
- **Salt and black pepper**
- **2 green onions, thinly sliced**

1. Bring large saucepan of salted water to a boil. Add noodles; return to a boil. Reduce heat to low. Cook 3 minutes or until tender. Drain and rinse under cold water to cool.
2. Heat oil in large skillet or wok over medium-high heat. Add mushrooms, bell pepper, dried chiles and garlic; cook and stir 3 minutes or until mushrooms are tender. Add cabbage; cover and cook 2 minutes or until cabbage is wilted.
3. Whisk broth, tamari and rice wine into cornstarch in small bowl until smooth; stir into vegetable mixture. Cook 2 minutes or until sauce is thickened.
4. Stir tofu and noodles into vegetable mixture; toss gently until heated through. Season with salt and black pepper. Sprinkle with green onions. Serve immediately.

Makes 4 servings

Vegetable Spaghetti Sauce with Meatballs

- **1 tablespoon olive oil**
- **1½ cups sliced white or cremini mushrooms**
- **½ cup plus 2 tablespoons finely chopped onion, divided**
- **½ cup chopped carrot**
- **½ cup chopped green bell pepper**
- **2 cloves garlic, minced**
- **1 can (28 ounces) diced tomatoes**
- **1 can (6 ounces) tomato paste**
- **2½ teaspoons Italian seasoning, divided**
- **1 teaspoon salt, divided**
- **¼ teaspoon black pepper**
- **1 egg**
- **2 tablespoons plain dry bread crumbs**
- **8 ounces ground beef**
- **12 ounces uncooked spaghetti**

1. Preheat oven to 375°F. Heat oil in large saucepan over medium heat. Add mushrooms, ½ cup onion, carrot, bell pepper and garlic; cook and stir 5 minutes or until vegetables are crisp-tender. Stir in tomatoes, tomato paste, 2 teaspoons Italian seasoning, ½ teaspoon salt and black pepper. Bring to a boil over medium-high heat. Reduce heat to medium-low; cover and simmer 20 minutes, stirring occasionally.
2. Combine egg, bread crumbs, remaining 2 tablespoons onion, ½ teaspoon salt and ½ teaspoon Italian seasoning in medium bowl. Add beef; mix until well blended. Shape into 16 meatballs. Place in 11×7-inch baking pan. Bake 18 to 20 minutes or until cooked through (160°F). Drain on paper towels.
3. Stir meatballs into sauce. Return sauce to a boil; reduce heat to low. Simmer, uncovered, about 10 minutes or until sauce thickens slightly, stirring occasionally.
4. Meanwhile, cook pasta in large saucepan of salted boiling water according to package directions for al dente. Drain and place in serving bowls; top with sauce and meatballs.

Makes 4 servings

SIDE DISHES

Wild Rice Mushroom Stuffing

- ½ cup uncooked wild rice
- Day-old French bread (about 4 ounces)
- ½ cup (1 stick) butter
- 1 large onion, chopped
- 1 clove garlic, minced
- 3 cups sliced mushrooms
- ½ teaspoon dried sage
- ½ teaspoon dried thyme
- ½ teaspoon salt
- ¼ teaspoon black pepper
- 1 cup vegetable broth
- ½ cup coarsely chopped pecans
- Fresh thyme sprigs (optional)

1. Prepare rice according to package directions. Preheat broiler.
2. Cut enough bread into ½-inch cubes to measure 4 cups. Spread in single layer on baking sheet; broil 5 inches from heat source 4 minutes or until lightly toasted, stirring after 2 minutes.
3. Melt butter in large skillet over medium heat. Add onion and garlic; cook and stir 3 minutes. Add mushrooms; cook 5 minutes, stirring occasionally. Add sage, dried thyme, salt, pepper and cooked rice; cook 2 minutes, stirring occasionally. Stir in broth. Add pecans and toasted bread cubes; toss gently. Transfer to 1½-quart casserole.* Preheat oven to 325°F.
4. Cover and bake 40 minutes or until heated through. Garnish with thyme sprigs.

**At this point, stuffing may be covered and refrigerated up to 8 hours before baking. Bake, covered, 50 minutes or until heated through.*

Makes 6 to 8 servings

Cheesy Spinach Casserole

1 pound baby spinach
4 slices bacon, chopped
1 small onion, chopped
1 cup sliced white mushrooms
¼ cup chopped red bell pepper
3 cloves garlic, minced
1½ teaspoons minced canned chipotle peppers in adobo sauce
1 teaspoon seasoned salt
8 ounces pasteurized process cheese product, cut into pieces
½ (8-ounce) package cream cheese, cut into pieces
1 cup thawed frozen corn
½ cup (2 ounces) shredded Monterey Jack and Cheddar cheese blend

1. Preheat oven to 350°F. Spray 1-quart baking dish with nonstick cooking spray.
2. Bring large saucepan of water to a boil over high heat. Add spinach; cook 1 minute. Drain and transfer to bowl of ice water to stop cooking. Drain and squeeze spinach dry; set aside. Wipe out saucepan with paper towel.
3. Cook bacon in same saucepan over medium-high heat until almost crisp, stirring frequently. Drain all but 1 tablespoon drippings from saucepan. Add onion to saucepan; cook and stir 3 minutes over medium heat or until softened. Add mushrooms and bell pepper; cook and stir 5 minutes or until vegetables are tender. Add garlic, chipotle peppers and seasoned salt; cook and stir 1 minute.
4. Add cheese product and cream cheese to saucepan; cook over medium heat until melted, stirring frequently. Add spinach and corn; cook and stir 3 minutes. Transfer to prepared baking dish; sprinkle with shredded cheese.
5. Bake 20 to 25 minutes or until cheese is melted and casserole is bubbly. If desired, broil 1 to 2 minutes to brown top of casserole.

Makes 6 servings

Red Cabbage with Bacon and Mushrooms

- **5 slices thick-cut bacon, chopped (about 8 ounces)**
- **1 onion, chopped**
- **1 package (8 ounces) cremini mushrooms, chopped (½-inch pieces)**
- **¾ teaspoon dried thyme**
- **½ medium red cabbage, cut into wedges, cored and cut crosswise into ¼-inch slices (about 7 cups)**
- **¼ teaspoon salt**
- **¼ teaspoon black pepper**
- **⅔ cup chicken broth**
- **3 tablespoons cider vinegar**
- **¼ cup chopped walnuts, toasted***
- **3 tablespoons chopped fresh parsley**

To toast walnuts, cook in small skillet over medium heat 4 to 5 minutes or until lightly browned, stirring frequently.

1. Cook bacon in large saucepan or skillet over medium-high heat until crisp. Remove from skillet with slotted spoon; drain on paper towels. Drain all but 1 tablespoon drippings from saucepan.
2. Add onion to saucepan; cook and stir 5 minutes or until softened. Add mushrooms and thyme; cook 6 minutes or until mushrooms begin to brown, stirring occasionally. Add cabbage, salt and pepper; cook 7 minutes or until cabbage is wilted.
3. Stir in broth, vinegar and half of bacon; bring to a boil. Reduce heat to low; cook, uncovered, 15 to 20 minutes or until cabbage is tender.
4. Stir in walnuts and parsley; sprinkle with remaining bacon.

Makes 6 servings

Green Bean Casserole with Homemade French Fried Onions

- **1 pound fresh green beans, cut into 2-inch pieces**
- **1 tablespoon vegetable oil**
- **1 package (8 ounces) cremini mushrooms, chopped**
- **3 tablespoons butter**
- **3 tablespoons all-purpose flour**
- **1 teaspoon salt**
- **¼ teaspoon red pepper flakes**
- **1 cup mushroom or vegetable broth**
- **1 cup whole milk**
- **Homemade French Fried Onions (recipe follows)**

1. Preheat oven to 350°F. Spray 13×9-inch baking dish with nonstick cooking spray.
2. Cook green beans in large saucepan of salted boiling water 4 minutes. Drain.
3. Heat oil in large saucepan over medium heat. Add mushrooms; cook and stir 8 minutes. Add butter; cook and stir until melted. Whisk in flour, salt and red pepper flakes. Gradually whisk in broth and milk; cook and stir until thickened. Remove from heat; stir in green beans. Pour into prepared dish.
4. Bake 30 minutes. Meanwhile, prepare Homemade French Fried Onions.
5. Remove casserole from oven. Top with onions; bake 5 minutes.

Makes 6 to 8 servings

Homemade French Fried Onions

- **2 small onions, sliced into rings**
- **½ cup milk**
- **½ cup cornstarch**
- **½ cup cornmeal**
- **1 teaspoon salt**
- **½ teaspoon black pepper**
- **Vegetable oil for frying**

1. Line baking sheet with paper towels. Separate onion rings and spread in shallow dish. Pour milk over onions; stir to coat. Combine cornstarch, cornmeal, salt and pepper in large bowl.
2. Heat 2 inches of oil in heavy skillet over medium-high heat to 325°F.
3. Working in batches, remove onion rings from milk to cornmeal mixture; toss to coat. Add onions to oil; fry 2 minutes per side or until golden brown. Remove to prepared baking sheet using tongs.

Makes about 1½ cups

Mushroom Quinoa

- **1 cup uncooked quinoa**
- **2 tablespoons olive oil, divided**
- **2 cups vegetable broth**
- **1 teaspoon poultry seasoning**
- **½ teaspoon salt**
- **1 small onion, diced**
- **1 package (8 ounces) cremini mushrooms, sliced**
- **8 ounces shiitake mushrooms, stemmed and sliced**
- **½ cup diced celery**
- **2 tablespoons chopped fresh parsley (optional)**

1. Place quinoa in fine-mesh strainer; rinse well under cold water.
2. Heat 1 tablespoon oil in medium saucepan over medium-high heat. Add quinoa; cook and stir until evenly coated. Stir in broth, poultry seasoning and salt. Bring to a boil. Reduce heat to low; cover and simmer 15 to 20 minutes or until quinoa is tender and broth is absorbed. Remove from heat.
3. Meanwhile, heat remaining 1 tablespoon oil in large skillet over medium heat. Add onion, mushrooms and celery; cook and stir 8 to 10 minutes or until vegetables are tender.
4. Combine quinoa and vegetables in large bowl. Sprinkle with parsley, if desired.

Makes 6 servings

Balsamic Roasted Vegetables

- **2 tablespoons butter, melted**
- **1 tablespoon olive oil**
- **1 tablespoon balsamic vinegar**
- **2 teaspoons honey**
- **1 teaspoon salt**
- **¾ teaspoon dried thyme**
- **¼ teaspoon black pepper**
- **1 large onion, cut into 1½-inch pieces**
- **2 red or yellow bell pepper (or one of each), cut into 1-inch pieces**
- **1 package (8 ounces) cremini or white mushrooms, thickly sliced**
- **2 carrots, cut diagonally into ¼-inch slices**
- **2 zucchini, cut into ½-inch slices**

1. Preheat oven to 425°F. Combine butter, oil, vinegar, honey, salt, thyme and ¼ teaspoon black pepper in small bowl; mix well.
2. Combine onion, bell pepper, mushrooms, carrots and zucchini on baking sheet. Drizzle butter mixture over vegetables; toss to coat. Spread vegetables in single layer.
3. Roast about 35 minutes or until vegetables are tender and beginning to brown and most liquid has evaporated, stirring halfway through cooking time.

Makes 6 servings

Zucchini Noodles with Roasted Garlic Cream Sauce

- 1 head garlic
- 2 tablespoons plus 1 teaspoon olive oil, divided
- 1 package (8 ounces) sliced mushrooms
- 1 medium zucchini, cut into ½-inch pieces
- 1¼ teaspoons salt, divided
- ½ teaspoon black pepper, divided
- 1 pound zucchini noodles
- 2 tablespoons butter
- 1 small onion, finely chopped
- ¼ cup dry white wine
- ⅓ cup whipping cream
- ¼ cup milk
- 1 tablespoon water
- 1 teaspoon cornstarch
- 1 cup (4 ounces) shredded white Cheddar cheese, plus additional for garnish
- ¼ cup grated Parmesan cheese
- 2 cups packed fresh spinach, stemmed

1. To roast garlic, preheat oven to 400°F. Cut off ½ inch from top of garlic head to expose cloves. Place on small sheet of foil; drizzle with 1 teaspoon oil. Wrap garlic with foil to enclose. Roast 35 to 40 minutes or until soft. Squeeze out roasted garlic from six cloves; chop or mash into paste. (Reserve remaining cloves for other recipes or spreading on bread.)

2. Heat large saucepan or Dutch oven over medium-high heat. Add mushrooms; cook about 8 minutes or until mushrooms release liquid and begin to brown, stirring occasionally. Add 1 tablespoon oil, chopped zucchini, ½ teaspoon salt and ¼ teaspoon pepper; cook about 5 minutes or until zucchini is crisp-tender, stirring occasionally. Transfer vegetables to large bowl; keep warm.

3. Add remaining 1 tablespoon oil, zucchini noodles and ¼ teaspoon salt to same saucepan; cook over medium-high heat 2 to 3 minutes or until noodles are slightly softened, stirring with tongs. Add to bowl with vegetables.

4. Melt butter in same saucepan over medium heat. Add onion; cook and stir 3 minutes or until translucent. Add mashed roasted garlic; cook and stir 1 minute. Add wine; cook 3 to 4 minutes or until almost evaporated, stirring occasionally. Stir in cream, milk, remaining ½ teaspoon salt and ¼ teaspoon pepper; bring to a simmer. Reduce heat to low; simmer 8 minutes, stirring occasionally.

5. Stir water into cornstarch in small bowl until smooth. Add to cream sauce; cook and stir over medium heat 1 minute or until thickened. Add 1 cup Cheddar and Parmesan by handfuls, stirring until blended before adding more cheese.

6. Add spinach and vegetable mixture to saucepan; toss gently to wilt spinach and coat vegetables with sauce. Season with additional salt and pepper to taste. Serve immediately with additional Cheddar, if desired.

Makes 2 main-dish or 4 side-dish servings

Oven-Roasted Vegetables

- **1 package (8 ounces) cremini mushrooms, halved or quartered if large**
- **8 ounces Brussels sprouts, trimmed and quartered**
- **2 carrots, diced (½-inch pieces)**
- **2 parsnips, diced**
- **1 medium red onion, diced**
- **1 medium zucchini, diced**
- **1 red bell pepper, diced**
- **2 tablespoons olive oil**
- **1 teaspoon salt**
- **¼ teaspoon black pepper**
- **1 tablespoon butter, melted**
- **1 green onion, finely chopped**
- **1 tablespoon chopped fresh basil**
- **1 clove garlic, minced**
- **1 tablespoon balsamic glaze**
- **1 tablespoon grated Parmesan cheese**

1. Preheat oven to 450°F. Combine mushrooms, Brussels sprouts, carrots, parsnips, red onion, zucchini and bell pepper in large bowl. Drizzle with oil; season with salt and pepper and toss to coat. Spread in single layer on baking sheet.
2. Roast 15 minutes. Stir vegetables; roast 5 to 10 minutes or until crisp-tender. *Turn oven to broil.*
3. Drizzle vegetables with butter; sprinkle with green onion, basil and garlic; stir to coat. Spread vegetables in single layer.
4. Broil 3 to 5 minutes or until edges of vegetables begin to brown. Drizzle with balsamic glaze; sprinkle with cheese.

Makes 4 servings

Five Mushroom Risotto

- 4 cups vegetable broth
- 4 tablespoons olive oil, divided
- 4 tablespoons butter, divided
- 1 shallot, minced
- ½ cup *each* shiitake, chanterelle, portobello, oyster and white mushrooms, wiped clean and chopped into ½-inch pieces
- 1 teaspoon salt, divided
- 1 cup uncooked arborio rice
- ¼ cup white wine
- ½ cup whipping cream
- ¼ cup grated Parmesan cheese
- ¼ cup fresh parsley, minced
- Salt and black pepper

1. Bring broth to a boil in medium saucepan over medium-heat heat. Reduce heat to low; keep warm.
2. Heat 2 tablespoons oil and 1 tablespoon butter in large saucepan over medium-high heat. Add shallot; cook and stir 2 to 3 minutes or until softened. Add mushrooms and ½ teaspoon salt; cook and stir until mushrooms have softened and reduced their volume by half. Transfer mushroom mixture to medium bowl.
3. Heat remaining 2 tablespoons oil and 1 tablespoon butter in same saucepan over medium-high. Add rice; cook and stir 2 minutes or until rice begins to turn translucent. Stir in wine and remaining ½ teaspoon salt; cook and stir 3 minutes or until wine is absorbed.
4. Reduce heat to medium. Add broth, ½ cup at a time, stirring frequently until broth is absorbed before adding next ½ cup. Continue adding broth and stirring until rice is tender and mixture is creamy, about 20 to 25 minutes.
5. Remove from heat. Add mushroom mixture, cream, Parmesan cheese and remaining 1 tablespoon butter; stir until cheese is melted. Stir in parsley. Season with additional salt and pepper.

Makes 4 servings

Veggie-Stuffed Portobello Mushrooms

- **4 large portobello mushrooms (1¼ to 1½ pounds)**
- **3 teaspoons olive oil or butter, divided**
- **1 cup chopped green or red bell pepper**
- **⅓ cup sliced shallots or chopped onion**
- **2 cloves garlic, minced**
- **1 cup chopped zucchini or yellow squash**
- **½ teaspoon salt**
- **¼ teaspoon black pepper**
- **1 cup panko bread crumbs or toasted fresh bread crumbs**
- **1 cup (4 ounces) shredded sharp Cheddar or mozzarella cheese**
- **Grated Parmesan cheese (optional)**

1. Preheat broiler. Line baking sheet with foil. Remove mushroom stems; chop and set aside. Scrape off gills from mushrooms caps with spoon and discard. Place mushrooms cap sides up on prepared baking sheet. Brush lightly with 1 teaspoon oil. Broil 4 to 5 inches from heat 5 minutes or until tender.

2. Meanwhile, heat remaining 2 tablespoons oil in large skillet over medium-high heat. Add bell pepper, shallots and garlic; cook and stir 5 minutes or until bell peppers begin to brown on edges. Stir in zucchini, chopped mushroom stems, salt and black pepper; cook and stir 3 to 4 minutes or until vegetables are tender. Remove from heat; cool 5 minutes. Stir in panko and Cheddar.

3. Turn mushroom caps over. Mound vegetable mixture into caps. Broil 2 to 3 minutes or until golden brown and cheese is melted. Sprinkle with Parmesan, if desired.

Makes 4 servings

Mushroom Gratin

- **4 tablespoons butter or olive oil, divided**
- **1 small onion, minced**
- **1 package (8 ounces) sliced cremini mushrooms**
- **2 cloves garlic, minced**
- **4 cups cooked elbow macaroni, rotini or other short pasta**
- **2 tablespoons all-purpose flour**
- **1 cup milk**
- **½ teaspoon salt**
- **½ teaspoon black pepper**
- **½ teaspoon dry mustard**
- **½ cup fresh bread crumbs**
- **1 tablespoon olive oil**

1. Preheat oven to 350°F. Spray shallow baking dish or casserole with nonstick cooking spray.
2. Melt 2 tablespoons butter in large skillet over medium-high heat. Add onion; cook and stir 2 minutes. Add mushrooms and garlic; cook and stir 6 to 8 minutes or until vegetables are soft. Remove from heat; stir in macaroni.
3. Melt remaining 2 tablespoons butter in medium saucepan over low heat. Whisk in flour; cook and stir 2 minutes without browning. Stir in milk; bring to a boil over medium-high heat, whisking constantly. Reduce heat to maintain a simmer. Add salt, pepper and mustard; whisk 5 to 7 minutes or until sauce thickens.
4. Pour sauce over mushroom mixture in skillet; stir to coat. Spoon into prepared baking dish. Top with bread crumbs; drizzle with oil.
5. Cover and bake 15 minutes. Uncover; bake 10 minutes or until bubbly and browned.

Makes 8 servings

Spinach and Bacon Salad

- **6 thin slices bacon, chopped**
- **¾ cup apple cider**
- **1 tablespoon plus 1 teaspoon rice wine vinegar**
- **¼ teaspoon salt**
- **¼ teaspoon black pepper**
- **6 cups packed fresh stemmed spinach**
- **1 cup sliced white mushrooms**
- **1 tomato, thinly sliced**
- **1 red onion, thinly sliced**

1. For dressing, cook bacon in medium skillet over medium-high heat 5 to 7 minutes until crisp, stirring occasionally. Remove half of bacon to small paper-lined plate with slotted spoon. Add apple cider, vinegar, salt and pepper to remaining bacon in skillet; cook and stir just until simmering. Remove from heat.
2. Combine spinach, mushrooms, tomato, onion and bacon in large bowl. Serve with dressing.

Makes 6 servings

Mediterranean Artichoke Salad with Rotini

- **1 cup uncooked rotini pasta**
- **1 can (14 ounces) quartered artichoke hearts, drained and coarsely chopped**
- **8 white mushrooms, thinly sliced**
- **1 tomato, chopped**
- **½ cup finely chopped red onion**
- **16 kalamata olives, pitted and coarsely chopped**
- **¼ cup chopped fresh parsley**
- **3 tablespoons white wine vinegar**
- **1 clove garlic, minced**
- **2 ounces crumbled feta cheese with sun-dried tomatoes and basil**

1. Cook pasta in large saucepan of salted boiling according to package directions for al dente. Drain and run under cold water until cool. Drain well.
2. Meanwhile, combine artichokes, mushrooms, tomato, red onion, olives, parsley, vinegar and garlic in medium bowl. Stir in pasta and feta cheese. Let stand 15 minutes for flavors to blend.
3. Serve immediately or cover and refrigerate up to 4 hours.

Makes 4 servings

Kale and Mushrooms with Bacon

- **1 slice bacon, chopped**
- **½ cup sliced shallots**
- **1 package (4 ounces) sliced mixed exotic mushrooms *or* 2 cups sliced cremini mushrooms**
- **10 cups (8 ounces) loosely packed torn stemmed kale leaves***
- **2 tablespoons water**
- **½ teaspoon black pepper**

Look for 16-ounce bags of ready-to-cook fresh kale leaves in the produce section of the supermarket.

1. Cook bacon in large skillet over medium heat 5 minutes. Add shallots; cook and stir 3 minutes. Add mushrooms; cook 8 minutes, stirring occasionally.

2. Add kale and water; cover and cook 5 minutes. Uncover; cook and stir 5 minutes or until kale is crisp-tender, stirring occasionally. Season with pepper.

Makes 4 servings

Mushroom Pilaf

- **2 tablespoons butter, divided**
- **1 package (3 ounces) soy flavor ramen noodles, crumbled**
- **½ cup chopped pecans**
- **1 package (8 ounces) sliced mushrooms**
- **2 cups hot cooked rice**
- **2 tablespoons chopped fresh parsley**

1. Melt 1 tablespoon butter in large skillet over medium-high heat. Add noodles and pecans; cook and stir 3 minutes or until toasted. Remove to plate.
2. Melt remaining 1 tablespoon butter in same skillet. Add mushrooms; cook 8 minutes or until browned, stirring occasionally.
3. Reduce heat to medium; add rice, ramen seasoning packet, noodle mixture and parsley; cook and stir 2 minutes or until heated through.

Makes 4 servings

Roasted Cremini Mushrooms with Shallots

- **1 pound cremini mushrooms, cut in half**
- **½ cup sliced shallots**
- **1 tablespoon olive oil**
- **½ teaspoon salt**
- **½ teaspoon dried rosemary**
- **¼ teaspoon black pepper**
- **Fresh rosemary sprigs (optional)**

1. Preheat oven to 400°F.
2. Spread mushrooms and shallots on large baking sheet. Whisk oil, salt, dried rosemary and pepper in small bowl. Pour over mushrooms and shallots; toss to coat evenly. Arrange in single layer on baking sheet.
3. Bake 15 to 18 minutes or until mushrooms are browned and tender. Garnish with fresh rosemary.

Makes 4 servings

Vegetables and Sun-Dried Tomatoes

- **1 pound green beans, ends trimmed**
- **1 tablespoon olive oil, divided**
- **4 ounces white or cremini mushrooms, thinly sliced**
- **½ cup sliced almonds**
- **½ cup sun-dried tomatoes (not packed in oil), sliced**
- **¼ teaspoon salt**

1. Cook green beans in large saucepan of salted boiling water 3 minutes. Drain.
2. Heat 2 teaspoons oil in large skillet over medium heat. Add green beans, mushrooms and almonds; cook and stir 3 minutes. Add remaining 1 teaspoon oil, sun-dried tomatoes and salt; cook and stir 2 minutes. Remove from heat, cover and let stand 15 minutes to absorb flavors.

Makes 4 servings

INDEX

INDEX

Metric Conversion Chart

VOLUME MEASUREMENTS (dry)

1/8 teaspoon = 0.5 mL
1/4 teaspoon = 1 mL
1/2 teaspoon = 2 mL
3/4 teaspoon = 4 mL
1 teaspoon = 5 mL
1 tablespoon = 15 mL
2 tablespoons = 30 mL
1/4 cup = 60 mL
1/3 cup = 75 mL
1/2 cup = 125 mL
2/3 cup = 150 mL
3/4 cup = 175 mL
1 cup = 250 mL
2 cups = 1 pint = 500 mL
3 cups = 750 mL
4 cups = 1 quart = 1 L

VOLUME MEASUREMENTS (fluid)

1 fluid ounce (2 tablespoons) = 30 mL
4 fluid ounces (1/2 cup) = 125 mL
8 fluid ounces (1 cup) = 250 mL
12 fluid ounces (1 1/2 cups) = 375 mL
16 fluid ounces (2 cups) = 500 mL

WEIGHTS (mass)

1/2 ounce = 15 g
1 ounce = 30 g
3 ounces = 90 g
4 ounces = 120 g
8 ounces = 225 g
10 ounces = 285 g
12 ounces = 360 g
16 ounces = 1 pound = 450 g

DIMENSIONS

1/16 inch = 2 mm
1/8 inch = 3 mm
1/4 inch = 6 mm
1/2 inch = 1.5 cm
3/4 inch = 2 cm
1 inch = 2.5 cm

OVEN TEMPERATURES

250°F = 120°C
275°F = 140°C
300°F = 150°C
325°F = 160°C
350°F = 180°C
375°F = 190°C
400°F = 200°C
425°F = 220°C
450°F = 230°C

BAKING PAN SIZES

Utensil	Size in Inches/Quarts	Metric Volume	Size in Centimeters
Baking or Cake Pan (square or rectangular)	8×8×2	2 L	20×20×5
	9×9×2	2.5 L	23×23×5
	12×8×2	3 L	30×20×5
	13×9×2	3.5 L	33×23×5
Loaf Pan	8×4×3	1.5 L	20×10×7
	9×5×3	2 L	23×13×7
Round Layer Cake Pan	8×1½	1.2 L	20×4
	9×1½	1.5 L	23×4
Pie Plate	8×1¼	750 mL	20×3
	9×1¼	1 L	23×3
Baking Dish or Casserole	1 quart	1 L	—
	1½ quart	1.5 L	—
	2 quart	2 L	—